PRAISE FOR *CRISIS AND RENEWAL*

"Steven Pan brings both heart and strategic acumen to *Crisis and Renewal.* A must-read for entrepreneurial leaders."

—**Steve Forbes,** Chairman and Editor-in-Chief, Forbes Media

"*Crisis and Renewal* is a story of courage and transformation. Steven Pan's journey resonates far beyond business—it speaks to the human spirit."

—**Michelle Yeoh,** Academy Award Winner, Global Humanitarian Advocate and UNDP Goodwill Ambassador

"Steven Pan's *Crisis and Renewal* offers a deeply human perspective on what it means to lead with values through times of upheaval. His story reflects the best of global entrepreneurship—rooted in heritage, shaped by resilience, and guided by a commitment to serve. This is a timely and inspiring memoir for anyone navigating complexity in a changing world."

—**Joe Tsai,** Chairman, Alibaba Group; Governor, Brooklyn Nets

"Steven Pan's *Crisis and Renewal* captures the courage and clarity required to lead through uncertainty. His passion for redefining luxury and his steadfast belief in the Regent vision helped turn challenge into opportunity. This memoir is an inspiring reflection on what it means to lead with heart, heritage, and a future-focused mindset."

— **Keith Barr,** Former CEO of InterContinental Hotels Group (IHG)

"Steven Pan's journey stands as a testament to resilience, culture, and purpose-driven reinvention. This is a timely and authentic account of transformative leadership. I especially appreciated his higher-order thinking and practice around culture. You will too."

—**Richard Lyons,** Chancellor of University of California, Berkeley

"Steven Pan's reflections in the book *Crisis and Renewal* remind us that leadership anchors in empathy, and the sense of purpose transforms adversity into strength. Taiwan, due to her unique geographical location and geopolitical environment since WWII, is an island of resilience. Steven Pan's book offers a moving story of overcoming challenges and striving for global presence with his business."

—**Mark Liu,** former Chairman of Taiwan Semiconductor Manufacturing Company (TSMC)

"*Crisis and Renewal* is a master class in leading through turbulence with empathy, courage, and purpose. Steven Pan offers the wisdom and personal reflection of a seasoned global entrepreneur and the heart of a human-centered leader. His story is an inspiring reminder that adversity, when met with compassion and resilience, can unlock extraordinary transformation."

—**Hubert Joly,** Harvard Business School, Former Best Buy CEO, Best-Selling Author, *The Heart of Business*

"Steven's life story is a testament to resilience and grace. Reading his journey has been nothing short of a blessing—an inspiration that stirs the soul and strengthens the heart, giving me renewed courage to meet life's trials and tribulations with hope and determination."

—**Walter Wang,** Founder, Chairman, and CEO of JM Eagle; Founder and Chairman, New Taipei Kings

"Steven Pan's reflections reveal how strong values and adaptive leadership can steer an organization through crisis toward global excellence. *Crisis and Renewal* is a thoughtful and timely contribution for leaders navigating complexity in any industry."

—**Cliff Oberlin,** Chairman & CEO of Oberlin Financial International and author of *Building a High-End Financial Services Practice* (Bloomberg Press, 2004) and *Family Fortunes – How Family Enterprises Thrive Across Generations* (2022)

"Steven Pan's journey with Regent Taipei is a powerful story of vision, resilience, and empathy. Rooted in Taiwan and shaped by both Eastern and Western values, he transformed some of the world's toughest crises into opportunities for growth. From pandemics to natural disasters, his leadership offers timeless lessons for navigating uncertainty with heart and purpose."

—**Syaru Shirley Lin,** Founder and Chair of Center for Asia-Pacific Resilience and Innovation

Crisis *and* Renewal

Crisis *and* Renewal

REFLECTIONS ON LEADERSHIP, EMPATHY, AND RESILIENCE BY A GLOBAL ENTREPRENEUR FROM TAIWAN

S. Steven Pan

with CHING-I LIN

TRANSLATED BY STACY A. MOSHER

Forbes | Books

Published by Forbes Books, Charleston, South Carolina.
An imprint of Advantage Media Group.

Printed in the United States of America.

10 9 8 7 6 5 4 3 2 1

ISBN: 979-8-88750-805-4 (Hardcover)
ISBN: 979-8-88750-806-1 (eBook)

Library of Congress Control Number: 2025918357

Back Flap and Interior Author Photo by Shing-I Chen.
Cover design by Matthew Morse.
Layout design by Lance Buckley.

08-29-2025 4:22

To all the Regents past, present, and future
who serve, stay, and celebrate with us:

Your trust makes our stewardship possible and
empowers our mission to bring the best of the
world to you, and the best of us to the world.

CONTENTS

PROLOGUE

Crisis as Catalyst

On April 3, 2024, a 7.4-magnitude earthquake struck Hualien County on Taiwan's eastern coast—roughly the same distance from the capital, Taipei, as Philadelphia is from New York City. The quake sent boulders tumbling from the soaring cliffs of Taroko National Park, one of Asia's most dramatic natural wonders. Landslides blocked mountain roads, stranding hundreds of people, including 319 guests and 125 staff of our hotel, Silks Place Taroko.

Another fifty hotel employees, including most of our management team, were commuting to work when the earthquake struck. With all cell phone towers down and communications severed, we had no idea what had happened to them. As the hours ticked by without word, it was impossible not to fear the worst.

Finally, at six o'clock that evening, three members of staff—Urza, Ken, and Jian Guo—arrived at the hotel, exhausted and covered in mud after climbing through rubble and navigating treacherous mountain paths. Beyond reporting that everyone on the hotel shuttles was safe, they'd had the presence of mind to document the contact information for twenty-nine stranded tourists, allowing us to notify anxious families worldwide. We also learned that our shuttle drivers had not only navigated their vehicles through falling debris but had also guided other travelers to safety beneath protective overhangs.

When military drones flew into the blocked canyon the next morning and transmitted footage of our stranded colleagues waving at the sky, many of us wept with relief after a sleepless night.

Over the next four days, as rescue crews cleared mountain roads, our Silks Place Taroko team demonstrated what decades of crisis management had taught us. Without senior management on-site or functioning communications, they organized themselves into an efficient emergency response unit. Recreation Manager Paula Wu, trained in search and rescue, coordinated with government teams and established a forward command post. Duty Supervisor Cece Wu managed guest services and kept our generators running. Medical specialist Chen Kuan-ting set up a field medical station and organized helicopter evacuations based on medical priority.

Our general manager (GM), Jackie Chao, had been in Taipei for a routine meeting when the earthquake struck. Rather than managing remotely, she returned to the hotel on April 7, hitching a ride with a construction crew willing to navigate the still-dangerous roads. While Jackie coordinated with rescue teams, our staff transformed the hotel into both fortress and sanctuary. The Central Emergency Operation Center landed helicopters on our lawn, and rescue workers—accustomed to harsh field conditions—were amazed when we provided hot showers, meals, and even laundry services. At the height of the crisis, our staff cared for nearly six hundred people with minimal outside contact.

Our international guests, many experiencing their first major earthquake, needed constant reassurance. Our staff set aside their own fears and exhaustion to provide round-the-clock support. They organized group activities to ease trauma, with our spa therapists offering complimentary treatments to stressed colleagues. In partnership with Buddhist Tzu Chi Hualien Hospital, we established an on-site counseling center providing psychological support and daily wellness checks.

This response wasn't extraordinary for our organization—it was business as usual. Our effectiveness stemmed from a simple principle that has guided our hotel group for three decades: Treat others as we wish to be treated. This golden rule, embedded in our DNA, ensures that in a crisis, every employee knows exactly what to do.

As I write this, Silks Place Taroko has finally reopened to the public in January 2025, after being closed for nine months. No employee has lost their job. Some remain on-site, helping with repairs; others are cross-training at sister properties. When we reopened, we emerged stronger—not despite the crisis but because of it.

This pattern of transformation through adversity defines the journey of Silks Hotel Group (SHG) from a single luxury property in 1990—Regent Taipei—to Taiwan's leading hospitality company, with annual operating profits exceeding US$100 million. Our philosophy rests on four pillars:

- Transform crisis into opportunity through empathetic leadership.
- Serve others as we wish to be served.
- Create sustainable value for all stakeholders.
- Bridge East and West, bringing the best of the world to Taiwan and showcasing the best of Taiwan to the world.

A Journey of Self-Transcendence

Mark Twain once warned that it's not what you don't know that gets you into trouble—it's what you know for sure that just isn't so. Business literature overflows with "rules for success," yet when applied to real experience, the rules' outcomes often differ dramatically from the promises.

The so-called rules for success often fall apart in real life because they reduce a complex journey to a simple formula. In truth, success depends less on following fixed steps and more on how people respond to both setbacks and lucky breaks. The ability to grow through those highs and lows—not just to endure them—shapes not only careers but also a deeper sense of meaning and purpose.

Another reason success is hard to copy is that people—and their circumstances—are always changing. What works for one person at one time may not work again, even for the same person. Those who achieve lasting success tend to adjust as they go. They don't cling to one way of doing things—they adapt, grow, and stay open to change. Progress often comes from this willingness to push beyond old habits through consistent effort.

Consider the butterfly, nature's symbol of transformation. The caterpillar must shed its skin multiple times before forming its chrysalis. Each molt represents risk—the vulnerable creature could be injured or devoured. Yet without these dangerous transformations, there can be no butterfly. Many ancient cultures recognized this truth, seeing the butterfly as representing the soul's journey toward rebirth.

In business, leaders who embrace continuous transformation can catalyze similar changes throughout their organizations. When this mindset permeates company culture, teams learn to see crisis not as threat but as opportunity for growth.

I've witnessed this principle transform my company, Regent Taipei, and the broader SHG. Over three decades, we've faced several existential threats: parent company bankruptcy in 2000, the SARS epidemic in 2003, the global financial crisis of 2008, and the COVID-19 pandemic. Each crisis brought chaos and doubt—and each revealed opportunities for profound transformation.

Success required more than weathering those storms; it demanded that we reimagine our business with each challenge. Through this process, we evolved from a single five-star hotel into an international hospitality group with multiple brands, including the international luxury Regent, the cultural luxury Silks, the hot-spring resort Wellspring, and the budget boutique Just Sleep.

The COVID-19 pandemic epitomized every crisis we'd faced. As competitors announced mass layoffs, we made a different choice. Guided by our principle of treating others as we wish to be treated, we announced that every employee would keep their job. This decision, seemingly unreasonable at a time of distress, sparked an innovation surge that made us the only profitable international hotel group in Taiwan during 2020, with net profits of US$24 million.

When Taiwan's strict lockdown banned indoor dining in May 2021, stripping revenues by 90 percent, we faced potential collapse. We immediately sold our Domino's Pizza franchise for US$57 million, securing resources to protect employees while accelerating digital transformation plans. As competitors struggled to rehire after the pandemic, we emerged fully staffed and stronger than ever. Prioritizing employee welfare proved to be my best business decision.

Like a butterfly emerging from its chrysalis, SHG transformed through crisis. Without those painful molts—each challenge forcing us to shed outdated thinking—we never would have unleashed our organization's true potential.

After three decades, I understand our mission clearly: Create harmony between culture, hospitality, and commerce that fosters both sustainable growth and human well-being. This principle of empathy now anchors every decision and offering across our hotel group.

Finding Purpose in Crisis

As Nietzsche wrote, "He who has a why to live can bear almost any how." Remarkable achievements require not just opportunity but also purpose—a reason for transformation that justifies the pain of change.

Even when we're surrounded by chances to grow, we often miss them, simply because we don't see their value right away. Moving forward—both as individuals and as a company—takes more than ambition. It takes clarity, steady effort, and a shared commitment to building something better together.

This book shares the business philosophy and life lessons that emerged from our journey through repeated crises. While rooted in hospitality, these insights apply beyond hotels. I won't focus on operational procedures but rather on leadership principles that foster transformation and growth in any organization.

This book serves readers who seek to understand

- how individuals and organizations evolve through crisis,
- the mindset needed to navigate transformative moments,
- how leaders can transcend conventional thinking, and
- why purpose and values matter more than profit in building sustainable success.

Corporations, like people, need reasons to exist beyond making money. Purpose allows organizations to transcend short-term pressures and focus on creating lasting value. Through these pages, I hope to encourage and empower readers to embrace transformation and build more sustainable, humane businesses.

I'll weave personal stories with objective analysis, creating a narrative that reflects the inseparable connection between human values and business success at Regent Taipei and SHG. My goal is to inspire others by showing how crisis can catalyze profound transformation, mutual prosperity, and genuine sustainability.

Regent Taipei is run like a Rubik's Cube with infinite business combinations and possibilities.

PART I

Transformation—Setting the Renaissance in Motion

CHAPTER 1

Foundations

To understand our transformation story, you need to know something about Taiwan—an island that embodies resilience itself. Located one hundred miles off China's coast, where the East and South China Seas meet, Taiwan packs twenty-three million people into a space smaller than Switzerland. This makes it one of earth's most densely populated places, yet also one of its most economically vibrant.

Taiwan's indigenous peoples share linguistic roots with Pacific islanders from the Philippines to Hawaii—evidence of ancient seafaring migrations. Despite lacking natural resources and facing frequent earthquakes and typhoons, Taiwan has built one of Asia's most dynamic economies.

The island's modern history reads like a chronicle of crisis and adaptation. After brief periods of Dutch and Spanish colonization in the 1600s, Taiwan became part of China's Qing dynasty. Japan took control after defeating China in a naval battle in 1895, ruling until World War II's end in 1945.

The next chapter proved even more dramatic. When Chiang Kai-shek's Nationalist government lost China's civil war to Mao Zedong's

Communists, two million soldiers, mandarins, and refugees—including my father—fled to Taiwan in 1949. They brought not just their lives but also six hundred thousand priceless artifacts from Beijing's Forbidden City, treasures now housed in Taipei's National Palace Museum.

This history created Taiwan's unique geopolitical position today. The People's Republic of China still claims sovereignty over Taiwan, while Taiwan has evolved into a vibrant democracy with strong ties to the United States. Despite facing an adversary 260 times its geographic size with 60 times its population, Taiwan hasn't just survived—it has thrived as an island of resilience and land of entrepreneurs.

Consider the challenges: expulsion from the United Nations (UN) in 1971, loss of US diplomatic recognition in 1979, the 1996 Taiwan Strait crisis when American aircraft carriers deterred Chinese military threats, and ongoing pressure today. Through it all, Taiwan's people and businesses learned to transform threats into opportunities.

Starting in the 1960s, Taiwan became the manufacturing hub for Silicon Valley as American tech giants outsourced production. By the 1990s, Taiwanese companies had become major investors in China itself. Today, Taiwan Semiconductor Manufacturing Company (TSMC) produces over 90 percent of the world's most advanced microchips, making Taiwan essential to everything from smartphones to artificial intelligence (AI).

This ability to transform adversity into advantage became the defining part of our hotel group's culture. Like Taiwan itself, Regent Taipei and SHG learned that lacking resources forces innovation, that constant threats build resilience, and that bridging cultures creates unique value.

In this context of perpetual challenge and adaptation, my father answered his nation's call to build Taiwan's first international hotel—planting the seed that would grow into today's SHG.

My Father: Answering the Call

Like me, my father, Pan Hsiao-Rui, was an unlikely hotelier. To the business world, he was a pioneer who helped build the island's postwar economy by recycling decommissioned naval vessels into valuable steel. He cofounded Nan Feng Steel Co., O-Ta Precision Industry Co., and eventually Regent Taipei while investing in major commercial real estate across Taiwan.

Born in 1924 in China's Fujian province, my father lost both parents before his teenage years, forcing him to raise his younger siblings alone. When Japan launched its full-scale invasion of China in 1937—including the horrific Nanjing Massacre—my father fled to southwest China to study mechanical engineering in Kunming, Yunnan province. As the Japanese army advanced in 1940, he evacuated with his entire school to Sichuan province, continuing his studies at Tongji University, one of China's top universities that had also relocated there to escape the war.

At just twenty years old, my father became the youngest major in Republic of China military intelligence, using his engineering skills to encode and decode secret communications—similar to the Navajo code talkers portrayed in American war films. His exceptional performance caught the attention of intelligence chief Dai Li, who promoted him to his personal staff.

After Japan's surrender in 1945, my father left military service and came to Taiwan in 1946 to work at an industrial facility in Kaohsiung. There, he met my mother, Huang Ya-Hsien, a meticulous accountant who had been one of the most popular students at Taiwan's top girls' school. It was love at first sight as they sat across from each other in the office. After marrying, they planned to start a trading and mercantile company, but China's civil war disrupted everything.

Me as an infant with my mother, Huang Ya-Hsien

Instead, they turned to an unexpected opportunity: salvaging scrap metal from ships the Japanese had scuttled in Taiwan's harbors during the war. This pivot proved prescient. Postwar Taiwan desperately needed steel for reconstruction but lacked natural resources. My father cofounded Nan Feng Steel Co., perfectly timed to meet this demand.

For the next three decades, my father traveled the world purchasing decommissioned naval vessels, accompanied by his translator, Peter Wang. Business boomed, and he earned the title "Taiwan's King of Shipbreaking." Taiwan dominated global ship recycling from the 1960s through the 1980s, providing crucial raw materials for the island's industrial development.

During the Korean and Vietnam Wars, my father became a major purchaser of surplus US military vessels. This relationship led to lucrative side businesses, including brokering electrical generators that the US military needed for its Vietnam bases.

One remarkable story illustrates his innovative spirit: When the US military decommissioned a ballistic missile propellant plant after switching from liquid oxygen to solid fuel in 1970, my father purchased the plant and towed the entire facility across the Pacific to Taiwan. Discovering local demand for industrial oxygen, he converted it into what became Taiwan's largest industrial gas company, later sold to LienHwa Industrial Holdings Corporation.

Another achievement was dismantling the iconic SS Nieuw Amsterdam, a thirty-seven-thousand-ton luxury liner that remains the largest ship ever scrapped in Taiwan. The vessel contained ten swimming pools and priceless art deco artwork—which my father unfortunately sold without proper appraisal.

Growing up around the shipbreaking business shaped both my brother, Roger, and me profoundly. We devoured Janes annual military reports that provide comprehensive information and specifications on the world's naval ships, aircrafts, and weapons systems. Roger developed a passion for art and antiques recovered from ships, becoming a prominent collector. I was captivated by military strategy, spending hours studying World War II history and playing war games with friends.

Looking back, my father's shipbreaking business taught me to find hidden value in what others discard and create new opportunities through creative repurposing—lessons that would prove invaluable in the hotel industry.

From Industrial Pioneer to Reluctant Hotelier

My father entered the hotel business in 1976 not by choice but in answer to his government's call during a national crisis. After Taiwan lost its UN seat to Communist China in 1971 and faced cascading diplomatic losses, foreign investors fled, fearing imminent Chinese takeover. President Chiang Ching-kuo launched an urgent campaign to restore international confidence by developing new industries that would attract foreign investment.

Taiwan had no international hotel sector—only the government-owned Grand Hotel served foreign visitors. To signal Taiwan's commitment to international business, the government recruited Robert B. Anderson, former US secretary of the Navy and the treasury and deputy secretary of defense, to invest in Taiwan's first international hotel. When Anderson needed a local partner, the US Navy recommended my father based on their long business relationship.

In Taiwan's first public–private partnership, the Anderson–Pan team signed a fifty-year lease for prime land in downtown Taipei, agreeing to pay 70 percent of market value. What should have been straightforward became an eight-year ordeal. The Taipei City Council blocked the budget to relocate existing squatters on the site, forcing my father to buy out each household individually. The clearance cost tripled the original lease payment, and, unable to use the land as collateral, my father sold family properties to raise funds.

Just as construction was finally ready to begin, Anderson withdrew, frustrated by years of delays. My father, equally exhausted, was relieved when Chen Yu-Hao of the Tuntex Group expressed interest in 1984. Chen purchased the majority stake of the project while insisting my father remain as minority partner. Together, they signed a management contract with Regent International Hotels. After six years of construction, Regent Taipei opened in 1990.

Reflecting on this venture, I wonder if my father would have proceeded in 1976 had he known the challenges ahead. Profit clearly wasn't his motivation—at the price he paid, he could have purchased what's now Taipei's entire central business district, Xinyi. He answered the government's call because Taiwan needed its first international hotel to restore investor confidence. Creating jobs and contributing to Taiwan's transformation from manufacturing to services mattered more than maximizing returns.

This pivot from shipbreaking to hospitality represents my father's ability to evolve with Taiwan's changing economy. His pioneering spirit ensured innovation became Regent Taipei's cornerstone from day one—a value now embedded in our organizational DNA.

Regent Taipei opening ceremony in 1990; (from left to right) Pan Hsiao-Rui, Chen Yu-Hao, and Regent Founder Robert Burns.

Regent Taipei was established during the tenure of Sun Yun-Suen as Premier of Taiwan's Executive Yuan. (Photographed on September 25, 1990, at the grand opening of the Regent Taipei)

The Two Faces of Empathy

Empathy drives innovation but manifests differently in business contexts. Strategic empathy—understanding others' motivations to gain advantage—dominates most commercial interactions. It's useful in negotiations, competition, and even poker, helping anticipate opponents' moves and minimize surprises.

But there's another kind: empathy aimed at mutual benefit, sometimes prioritizing others' needs above our own. While my father certainly employed strategic empathy as a successful businessman, it was his selfless version that shaped my leadership philosophy.

Despite building a business empire, my father never forgot his impoverished youth. Soon after achieving success, he established the Hsiang-Ho Education Foundation, channeling millions of US dollars to education, disaster relief, and social services across Taiwan for decades.

He set a family rule: Share generously in good times and be self-reliant in bad times without burdening others. Even as a shipping magnate, he maintained the same circle of old friends, hand-washed his own clothes, and prepared his own breakfast. When I once tried to buy him a new desk, he set an impossibly low budget of fifty US dollars. I found a solid wood piece that exceeded his limit, convincing him to take it only by claiming it was secondhand.

This unusual combination of personal frugality and boundless public generosity defined him. His childhood struggles to obtain an education made him a fierce advocate for equal access to learning. His foundation provided scholarships throughout Taiwan and funded universities, including Fo Guang University and University of the West in California.

What I admired most in my father was how he viewed success as an opportunity to help others succeed. When diagnosed with early-onset dementia in his later years, he not only cured himself through determination and experimental cocktail drug treatment but founded Hsiang Ho Biotech to make the supplement available to others. The company's model: Donate one bottle to low-income patients for every bottle sold retail. He pioneered *social enterprise* before the term existed in Taiwan.

Looking back, I see how my father embedded these values into Regent Taipei from its founding. His empathetic approach—treating others with the kindness and respect he'd want—gave him strength through early hardships and guided his transformation from poverty to prosperity. When you have nothing, your beliefs become your strength. Having experienced deprivation, he dedicated himself to serving the disadvantaged and creating opportunity for all.

This same empathy now permeates every aspect of Regent Taipei and SHG, guiding how we approach guests and employees with compassion, understanding, and service—an approach that creates positive impact far beyond our hotels.

Pan Hsiao-Rui was always answering the call for greater good in areas where the country needed him the most, beginning with his military service and followed by his shipbreaking venture, the founding of Regent Taipei, and philanthropic initiatives that expressed his unwavering dedication to Taiwan.

Culture Eats Strategy for Breakfast

Over two decades, I've made it my mission to weave empathy into Regent Taipei's cultural fabric. Genuine empathy can't be faked—it shapes how we live and work, creating consistency between professional and personal values that becomes invaluable in corporate culture.

A pivotal 2013 conversation with UC Berkeley's Haas School of Business Dean Richard Lyons (later chancellor) reinforced this belief. We discussed the school's four leadership principles: Question the Status Quo, Confidence Without Attitude, Students Always, and Beyond Yourself. His insights confirmed what experience had taught me: Culture trumps strategy, especially in crisis. The values anchoring corporate culture must be sacrosanct, impervious to opportunism and market volatility.

Hotels succeed through more than guest service and fine dining. Success requires orchestrating countless support functions—kitchens, housekeeping, maintenance, reservations, marketing, finance, HR, purchasing, engineering, IT, laundry—each demanding unique expertise. Any breakdown ruins the guest experience. Unlike manufacturing, where defects can be tolerated at certain rates, hotels operate in a zero-sum environment where the slightest misstep becomes service failure.

At Regent Taipei, we expect more than technical competence. Our team welcomes and serves people from diverse cultures with intuitive empathy that shapes every guest interaction. Like gracious hosts at an elegant dinner party, every employee plays a vital role in making guests feel genuinely valued.

What does this cohost role mean? It's being present yet unobtrusive, like shadows complementing sunlight. The best service remains invisible until needed.

Many employees' touching stories illustrate this philosophy. When a housekeeping staff member learned that an American guest had a severe cold, she prepared her family's special chicken soup and delivered it personally. While not standard procedure, this gesture perfectly conveyed our desire for the guest's recovery while giving someone who'd experienced five-star hotels worldwide a taste of uniquely Taiwanese hospitality. Such kindness creates ripple effects throughout our hotels, embedding itself in SHG's DNA.

Psychologist Irvin Yalom defined empathy clinically as "looking out from the other's window"—seeing the world through their eyes.[1] In business, empathy means viewing situations from all stakeholders' perspectives to create mutually beneficial solutions.

Empathy drives organizational success by fostering shared purpose and values. Leading with empathy inspires teams to act in everyone's best interest, creating sustainable momentum. We treat all stakeholders—guests, employees, shareholders, partners—as we wish to be treated.

This approach bridges perspectives, helping us understand and value others' experiences. At its deepest level, empathy creates connection with the broader world, even fostering a sense of universal unity. This awareness helped me understand why my father emphasized helping others on the path to success. I've learned that empowering others brings more meaning and reward than simply writing checks.

Finding My Own Path

Three decades leading Regent Taipei and SHG has transformed not just our organization but also my entire philosophy of business and life. I've learned that hospitality isn't merely a service industry—it's a process of combining aesthetics with a global perspective to lift human experience: Serve to move the world. My childhood explorations and opportunities proved essential in reaching this understanding.

1 Irvin Yalom, *The Gift of Therapy: An Open Letter to a New Generation of Therapists and Their Patients* (Harper Perennial, 2017).

My favorite childhood toys were model trains my father would bring me from his overseas travels, along with my extensive LEGO collection. These became creative portals, instilling a lifelong fascination with architectural design.

My brother Roger, fourteen years older than me, ignited my passion for music. He trained me as a DJ for summer parties at our Kaohsiung home when I was just five or six, spinning classic Western pop. Roger also shared his military-history expertise and love of antiques.

My sister Pi-Ching, ten years my senior, shaped my international outlook and intellectual development. Our desks that faced each other meant I absorbed wisdom from her studies of Don Quixote and Shakespeare, building my English foundation.

Growing up in an affluent household, I was raised primarily by Grandma Huang after my mother's health declined following multiple pregnancies. Grandma instilled fierce frugality even amid plenty, teaching that wasting earth's resources was unforgivable. She separated tissue paper to use each layer individually—a conservation ethic that would fit perfectly in today's sustainability movement.

I was about to start high school when the US severed diplomatic relations with Taiwan in 1979, triggering widespread panic about the island's future. When I was fifteen, my father sent me to live with my brother, Roger, and his wife, Nancy, in San Francisco. Nancy, though raising her own children, treated me like family. Her warm hospitality and delicious home cooking left deep impressions on me about creating welcoming environments.

Living in America transformed my relationship with my father. Though we'd barely interacted in Taiwan—he was always traveling for business—we began corresponding regularly. He visited annually, and through Roger's subscription to Taiwan's *Wealth Magazine* (their

Forbes equivalent), I learned more about his business empire than I'd ever known at home.

As the youngest son, I initially wanted to study architecture in college, drawn to creative design. Then I switched to premed at the University of Michigan, only to discover that I couldn't stand the sight of blood. Finally, I transferred to UC Berkeley to study economics. Each shift shed one of my identity layers while retaining valuable perspectives—my genetics and evolutionary biology studies later guided biotechnology and healthcare investments.

To make up for time lost during earlier detours, I decided to skip part-time work at Berkeley and focus entirely on finishing my degree as quickly as possible. That meant sticking to a tight budget, since my family's financial support covered only the basics. Luckily, I had already learned the value of saving from Grandma Huang. When I was a kid, I'd come home from school hungry and craving my favorite snack: a scallion pancake with egg. But I noticed the street vendor charged much more for the egg than it cost at home, so I started bringing my own. Handing over the egg saved me money—and still gave me the satisfaction of enjoying the full version of my favorite snack for the price of a plain one.

At Berkeley, fitting a car into my budget required extreme sacrifice. I rented a room, which was simply a converted balcony, for one hundred dollars monthly. It was comfortable in the summer but miserable in the winter, as mold crept through the thin walls. I endured until I found an affordable apartment to share.

My active engagement in campus activities is how I crossed paths with my future wife, Constance. One day, while people-watching with my roommate, Alex, on campus, I spotted a beautiful, ethereal girl passing by, and it was love at first sight. At that moment, I turned to Alex and said, "She is gonna be my wife."

Fate intervened months later at a career recruiting event where Constance was moderating. I made a terrible first impression, grabbing food before the event started. She stopped me, explaining that the food was for after the event. At least I had found a way of ensuring she'd remember me!

As it happened, we were both economics majors. My study strategy involved intense listening during lectures and doing library research on likely exam topics, avoiding textbooks or notes. Constance took meticulous notes, which she let me review before exams. This approach earned consistently high grades, and I graduated early from Berkeley with a bachelor's degree in economics.

After graduation, Constance became a financial analyst at Macy's in New York while I pursued an MBA at Columbia University. Her unwavering support allowed me to completely focus on my studies. When I had completed my degree, we got married at twenty-three in San Francisco's Grace Cathedral. My brother drove us; my best man, Kevin Wu, my high school classmate and the very first friend that I made in the United States, forgot our rings and had to race home—which became an enduring joke among friends. A longtime friend and partner, Kevin has managed our US commercial real estate business for three decades, encompassing some of the most iconic corporate headquarters transactions involving Chevron and Apple Computer.

I began postgraduate life at my dream firm, First Boston (later Credit Suisse), applying my financial training at one of Wall Street's premier investment banks. But instead of guiding me to my long-term future, this became another transition point in my life.

Working on Wall Street, I began to reflect on my prospects. I realized that single-minded pursuit of wealth left little room for happiness or fulfillment. Financial success wasn't my ultimate goal but a means to greater ends. By twenty-five, I'd accumulated enough wealth for comfortable living compared to my frugal upbringing with Grandma Huang, yet I felt unfulfilled.

Homecoming to Destiny

As I reached this new inflection point in 1991, Regent Taipei announced the need for a full-time president. My father had founded the hotel but wasn't directly involved in operations. My brother, Roger, served as president part-time, but his expanding Chinese investments prevented proper attention to Taipei's newest luxury property once it opened in 1990.

Chen Yu-Hao, my father's partner and Regent Taipei's chairman, approached me with an offer. As the founder's son with Wall Street finance experience, I seemed the natural choice to expand the business beyond a single hotel and take the company public.

I accepted the offer out of loyalty to my father, though returning to Taiwan wasn't easy. Constance had been born and raised in America and spoke little Chinese. American life was all she knew. After I promised that our Taiwan stint would be temporary, she joined me two years later. Our children eventually grew up in Taiwan before attending American universities, making our "temporary" assignment permanent.

This homecoming began my transformation from Wall Street associate to hospitality leader, setting the stage for three decades of crisis, growth, and the discovery that true success comes not from maximizing shareholder value but from creating sustainable benefits for all stakeholders—employees, guests, partners, and community.

The lessons my father embedded in Taiwan's first international hotel would guide us through challenges that threatened our existence yet ultimately made us stronger, teaching that empathy and cultural bridging create value far beyond financial returns.

Regent City: More Than a Building

Over time, I came to realize that Regent Taipei is not just a building but a miniature city that runs twenty-four hours a day. Like any city, it contains residential areas (guest rooms), commercial districts (restaurants and shops), infrastructure (engineering, security, IT), and administration (finance, HR, marketing). It connects with customers and employees across continents while sourcing materials globally for services and maintenance.

The hotel industry's symbiotic relationship with more than four hundred other sectors makes each property like a massive Rubik's Cube with countless moving parts. Any misalignment affects the whole. This complexity demands constant innovation. With this in mind, it is easier to appreciate how innovation has been woven into the very fabric of Regent Taipei.

We were Taiwan's first five-star hotel to include luxury shopping. We also pioneered operating restaurants and rooms as independent profit centers, allowing each unit to optimize its performance and develop unique brand identities. This business-model innovation predated similar moves by international hotel chains by decades.

As Executive Chairman of SHG, I've navigated numerous near-disasters. But these close calls became a source of inspiration. They taught me how strategic shifts can transform potential catastrophe into competitive advantage. SHG's reputation as Taiwan's leading hotel group rests not only on consistent profitability but also on remarkable resilience through repeated crises.

Despite challenges over three decades, the Regent Taipei Rubik's Cube always regained balance, shook off debris, and moved forward. I see myself less as hotel owner than as value cocreator on a lifestyle platform spanning dining, accommodation, shopping, culture, and learning. Managing Regent Taipei as an "invisible city" created unique spaces for exploring hospitality aesthetics across all services.

Our hotel offers visitors multicultural experiences that are unavailable in everyday life. With every crisis recovery and reconfiguration, SHG has opened new chapters in its own story and written a new page in Taiwan's hospitality history.

My brother Roger's Chinese name, Sy-Zuan, derives from the proverb, "When drinking water, contemplate its source"—remember where blessings originate. My father never explained my Chinese name, Sy-Lian, but it evokes the Latin phrase *fiat lux*, which means *let there be light*. In hindsight, this perfectly captures my experience leading Regent Taipei through crises: Always seek the illumination beyond darkness.

Bringing Humanity into Business

Leading SHG through times of crisis has shown me that being there—and standing by our people—makes all the difference when it comes to long-term resilience. I have taken inspiration from John Hennessy, the respected academic and business leader, who emphasizes how crucial it is for leaders to show empathy, act with courage, and stay attuned to others' needs when things get tough. But those lessons didn't just come from books—I first learned them by watching my father, who lived them every day.

I have also learned that a leader's personal growth must sync with company development, and this has motivated me to deepen my understanding of business across related fields and international relations.

Recognizing that business success extends beyond boardrooms, I frequently share insights at international conferences about hospitality, investment, and leadership. I joined the Young Presidents'

Organization (YPO), which provides a global platform for business leaders to develop through lifelong learning and networking.

When COVID-19 devastated Taiwan's hotels, our flagship hotel, Regent Taipei, faced massive losses. Rather than cut staff or salaries, I announced we'd redirect all energy toward transforming Regent Taipei into an innovative urban resort for domestic tourism. By confronting the pandemic head-on, we transformed potential disaster into opportunities for personal, professional, and corporate growth, creating a positive case study for the global hospitality industry.

Each challenge Regent Taipei has faced has presented opportunities to sharpen our competitive edge. Establishing SHG transformed hotel management into change management, making us embrace change as a catalyst for growth. But while techniques change, philosophy must remain steadfast. Changing methods without adhering to a fundamental philosophy prevents current changes from inducing further transformation.

This eternal inquiry—from business to business philosophy—challenges leaders and enterprises, just as individuals seeking fulfilling lives must know themselves completely. Solving practical problems requires that we first understand ourselves.

Crisis is a catalyst for self-examination, offering the best opportunity for breakthrough self-awareness and growth. It challenges preconceptions and uncovers new perspectives. Regent Taipei's first thirty-year journey encompasses three major transformations which will be explained in the following chapters.

CHAPTER 2

First Transformation

(1998–2003)

The five years from 1998 to 2003 were marked by a series of crises and challenges that would set the stage for our hotel group's first major transformation. My battle for control of Regent Taipei amid a global economic downturn led to the launch of the asset-light business model that became a new trend among Taiwan's listed companies, which were typically overcapitalized and asset-intensive.

Soon after Regent Taipei went public in 1998, the mainland-China investments of Tuntex Group began to flounder during the Asian financial crisis. This put financial strain on Tuntex and Regent Taipei Chairman Chen Yu-Hao, who proposed that Regent Taipei purchase Tuntex Group's real estate investment in Beijing as a bailout strategy. Twenty years ago, corporate governance concepts had not yet reached maturity in Taiwan, and as a result, related-party transactions of this kind remained common.

As Regent Taipei's president, and someone trained in corporate finance and governance ethics through my American MBA education, I firmly rejected this investment. "We don't do deals with our own companies," I said. "In particular, this kind of ethically compromised proposal goes against everything the Pan family stands for."

Chen had no intention of backing down, however, and after I voiced my opposition, he proposed a special motion in a board meeting that I be removed as president. It was only through the strenuous objections of my father that the board delayed the motion for my removal. Even so, I was forced to go on extended leave. At that time, Independent Board Supervisor T. J. Huang passed me a note consisting of two words: Be patient.

T. J. Huang's support was critical for me at this time. My father, although agreeing with me in principle, was in favor of letting Chen have his way rather than creating animosity with a powerful adversary, and many other members of the board were also inclined that way. I could only count on T. J.'s integrity, and I went back to the United States with my family.

Three months later, Chen once again pushed for Regent Taipei's buyout of the Tuntex Beijing property, but T. J. Huang countered him by requiring anyone on the board with an interest in Tuntex to abstain from voting. As a result, Regent Taipei's board of directors scrapped the plan. By the time I returned to Regent Taipei, I had gained important insights into the massive gulf between the business philosophies of the two sides, in particular, the often blurry boundaries between personal and company interests of powerful local conglomerates such as Tuntex. This understanding informed the next phase of my journey in the corporate world. For the next two years, I fought Chen by attempting to put in place corporate governance measures to stop conflicts of interest and related-party transactions, with the help of my Chinese American council Nicholas Chen of Pamir Law and Robert Huang, despite his incomparably greater financial prowess and experience.

The financial crisis that the Tuntex Group experienced in 2000 had a far-reaching impact because Regent Taipei and Tuntex had a fifty-fifty joint venture in a mega mixed-use hotel retail complex in Taichung. Since Regent Taipei jointly owned the complex with Tuntex and served as coguarantor for its bank loans, Regent faced imminent financial distress as both Tuntex and the Taichung complex continued their downward spiral. I recognized that I was Regent Taipei's last line of defense in surviving Tuntex's financial crisis.

Determined to save the hotel my father had founded and to protect the jobs of our thousands of employees, I formed a coalition of foreign investors and overseas banks. Putting my family's entire financial stake in the company up as collateral, I put together an investor group to acquire Tuntex's more than 50 percent stake in Regent Taipei at a 30 percent premium above market value, for a total transaction value of nearly NT$5 billion (approximately US$170 million at the time). In return, Tuntex agreed to acquire Regent Taipei's 50 percent stake in the Taichung Complex at a 50 percent discount—for a total cost of around NT$1 billion—which ended Regent Taipei's responsibility as a joint guarantor on the loan. My decision was vindicated shortly thereafter: The Tuntex Group declared bankruptcy in 2001, with debts totaling an estimated NT$60 billion and the equity value of the Taichung complex reduced to zero.

However, that wasn't the last challenge we faced during that period. On September 11, 2001, terrorists attacked the United States at multiple sites, causing thousands of fatalities. The devastating destruction of the Twin Towers of the World Trade Center in New York City was a major shock to the US economy and global travel, which was reflected in Regent Taipei's collapsing stock price. The shares I had recently purchased from the Tuntex Group at NT$25 each were now valued at less than NT$10. For the Pan family, it was like being on margin call day after day. But the crisis presented an opportunity to rethink our capital-intensive business model.

In 2002, I made an unprecedented move for a listed company in Taiwan by embarking on a major capital restructuring journey toward an asset-light model that would benefit both the company and its investors. The experience of the joint venture with Tuntex on the Taichung Hotel Complex had soured me for life on tying up massive amounts of capital in brick-and-mortar assets. The project had lost money consistently since its opening in 1988 and had dragged down the finances of both of its parent companies in the process.

At the same time, I observed that overseas, leading hotel chains such as Marriott and Hyatt were shifting their portfolios to focus 99 percent on hotel management and branding rather than ownership of fixed assets. This trend hadn't yet caught on in Taiwan, but I saw its general principles as a way out for our hotel business. Clearly, the future lay in managing hotels and brands, rather than sinking huge amounts of money into cumbersome physical structures.

Determined not to repeat the Taichung debacle but also needing to decide what to do with the cash on hand, I decided to apply the principle of corporate finance 101 and redistribute our excess cash reserves to our shareholders. I explained the logic of an asset-light focus to our board of directors: "Of course, it would be possible to invest idle cash in new investments, but wouldn't it be better to focus on our core business and return this cash to our shareholders so they can make their own investments?"

Halving our cash reserves from NT$4.3 billion to NT$2.1 billion made Regent Taipei the first profitable, publicly traded company in

Taiwan to reduce its capital while raising its earnings per share (EPS) and return on equity. In the past, listed companies had only reduced their capital because they were losing money. Our action was so unprecedented that when Regent Taipei CFO Dick Lin submitted the documents to Taiwan's Financial Supervisory Commission, he was required to sign a guarantee for the company as a going concern. We found this a winning strategy and set a new precedent and role model for corporate governance and shareholder value maximization in Taiwan. After that, numerous other major companies—such as Chunghwa Telecom, China Telecom, YAGEO, Taiwan Mobile, and Realtek—adopted a similar approach to strengthen their overall financial structure.

By now, I was committed to the strategy of transforming the traditional logic of the hotel business from ownership to management and focusing on building the brand rather than more hotels. The success of the company's capital restructuring was reflected in its rising stock price and market prospects.

Then, just as the hotel industry recovered, the SARS pandemic hit in 2003. Once again, tourism and business travel plummeted worldwide, especially in East Asia, as governments struggled to cope with this unprecedented threat. Regent Taipei's revenues dropped by half within days of the outbreak.

Revolutionary Innovation: The Profit Center System

External crises tested our resolve at a time when we were already undergoing an internal transformation that would fundamentally reshape our operations. Shortly after becoming president of Regent Taipei in 1991, I faced my first major challenge: implementing Chairman Chen's vision of a profit center system. Chen was convinced that hotels could greatly benefit from adopting profit center principles similar to those successfully used by his industrial Tuntex Group.

Introducing the profit center concept, though common in manufacturing and traditional industries, represented a management revolution for hotels and the broader service industry. Regent Taipei became the first hotel in Taiwan—and perhaps the world—to adopt such a model, placing us at the forefront of innovation in hospitality management.

Every management system has its advantages and disadvantages. Hotels traditionally operate under a centralized structure where the general manager (GM) is like the captain of a ship, ensuring efficient and absolute management. While the nature of the industry prioritizes on-the-spot decision-making, this easily develops into a complacent mentality and hidden costs that aren't accurately reflected in operational performance. The result is a tendency to waste food, energy, and other resources. The profit center system is more granular, decentralizing the entire hotel into small business units and placing emphasis on the empowerment of lower-level managers. The difference between the two systems is significant, and adopting the profit center system required launching a wholesale organizational reform.

Let's consider the food and beverage (F&B) department as an example. In the traditional hotel setup, chefs are led by the executive chef, and internal reports are generated within the executive chef's office. However, with the introduction of profit centers, each restaurant within the hotel operates as an independent entity with its own financial statements, and the chefs are held accountable to the restaurant manager instead of the executive chef. This requires redesigning organizational reporting lines and jobs.

To assist me in this endeavor, Chairman Chen enlisted the expertise of Huang Ben-Ming, an industrial engineering specialist from Tuntex. Like most five-star hotels, Regent Taipei had a central kitchen, so the two of us began by examining the kitchen's workflow—as observers, not cooks. Employing operational management techniques, we calculated the time and cost taken up by each restaurant. This allowed us to deduce cost-distribution formulas that more clearly reflected the actual performance of each individual restaurant.

The introduction of the profit center system was undoubtedly one of the most challenging moments in my life up to that time. Resistance resounded throughout the hotel, from the top managers down to the cooks. Even the foreign GM expressed concern, saying, "I might be out of a job soon!" With every profit center run by its own leader, it seemed as if everyone had become a small boss.

In fact, a GM has many responsibilities. Along with overseeing the collaboration of different departments, they are in charge of quality control. While the profit center system encouraged cost control, this pursuit of cost efficiency could not overshadow the commitment to maintaining exceptional guest experiences. The GM therefore became responsible for upholding the highest standard of overall quality control and setting the culture of excellence in the hotel.

During this transformative period, every unit capable of generating revenue became an independent profit center, including the laundry room, flower shop, and fitness center. We divided the hotel into more than twenty distinct profit centers, each devising its own employee structure and producing financial reports that enabled us to measure operational performance and allocate bonuses accordingly.

As we progressed, we categorized profit centers as large, medium, and small. For instance, Regent Taipei's first-floor restaurants were amalgamated into a medium-sized profit center, while the external Spice Market and Silks Palace restaurants each became additional medium-sized profit centers. Even the guest room department was further subdivided into units, such as the business center, telecommunication services, and executive lounge—each constituting a small profit center.

Building Fair Systems

In the manufacturing industry, implementing profit centers enables evaluating the performance of individual units. It's more challenging to implement in the service industry, however, because hotels include many public spaces and shared resources that are difficult to evaluate on their own. We therefore had to spend a great deal of time configuring an appropriate model.

For example, to which profit center should the cost of the live band in the hotel's atrium be assigned? Should all of the hotel's restaurants share the cost, even the restaurants where the band cannot be heard? And how should we allocate the maintenance costs of public areas, such as the lobby and restrooms?

We had to consider all aspects of the hotel's brand image and overall guest experience in order to make a fair and equitable decision. After much deliberation, we decided that the atrium performances were an integral part of our brand image and guest experience. To determine the cost-sharing for each profit center, we used a weighted system similar to the pricing of tickets for different sections in a concert hall. Profit centers closer to the stage area carried a higher weight, while those farther away had a lower weight. We treated the hotel lobby as a storefront, and since it was located on the second floor, that floor became the prime rent location, with the rent ratio decreasing on higher and lower floors.

Cost sharing for cleaning and maintaining restrooms was calculated based on the number of guests. Three profit centers located on the second floor—Robin's Grill, Robin's Teppanyaki, and the Gallery

Lounge—shared the cost of cleaning and maintenance of restrooms on that floor based on their respective customer counts.

We also created profit centers in our logistical departments, including public relations (PR), accounting, and HR. The cost allocation for these departments was calculated based on revenue, square footage, and the number of employees. Since the HR department served the entire group, calculations were based on the number of employees in each unit.

Regent Taipei currently has profit centers for its guest rooms, first and second floors, refrigerated beverages department, spa, various external restaurants, Just Sleep hotels, and so on. Implementing the profit center system was no easy feat, however, and it took several years of adjustments, modifications, and fine-tuning to make it work.

One major challenge in implementing profit centers in hotels is dealing with shared spaces and resources. For example, the live band performances in the atrium are an integral part of the hotel's brand image and contribute to the overall guest experience. To allocate the costs of these performances to each profit center, a weighted calculation method allocates a higher percentage of the cost to profit centers closer to the atrium area analogous to concert ticketing.

Another crucial aspect of the profit center system goes beyond simply examining each unit's revenue and costs. It involves evaluating the operational performance from a financial perspective that focuses on the bottom line. This approach reveals important insights into the hidden costs within the organization. A prime example is the hotel's limousine department.

Taking the lead from Regent Hong Kong's Rolls-Royce shuttle service, Regent Taipei operated a limousine department that chauffeured guests in stretched Cadillacs when it opened in 1990.

After we began implementing the profit center system, we found that the limousine department had a low utilization rate that didn't justify the cost of maintaining more than ten limousines and a staff of more than twenty drivers on a rotating schedule. If treated as an independent profit center, it would have incurred annual losses. On that basis, we decided to outsource our limousine service to a reputable limousine company. Regent Taipei allocated four parking spaces to the company and insisted on the same model, year, and quality of vehicles to maintain our high standards and ensure that our guests remained satisfied. The limousine operation has been profitable ever since.

Each profit center operates with its own balance sheet, requiring the effective control of costs and expenses relative to revenue. A crucial consideration in this system is internal transfer pricing, so ensuring the success of the profit center system requires not only strong leadership but also establishing reasonable and fair rules of the game.

In this intricate web of operations, each unit may act as both buyer and seller to other units within the organization, so clear and transparent accounting practices are essential for seamless operations. For instance, when the Chinese restaurant orders desserts from the central kitchen, it takes the role of buyer, while the kitchen assumes the role of seller. The seller will naturally aim for a higher price, while the buyer seeks a lower price. This raises the question of how to determine the internal transfer price of the dessert.

Through a series of meticulous tests and evaluations, Regent Taipei established an internal transfer price system firmly anchored to market prices. This means that the central kitchen is competing with restaurants and dessert shops beyond the hotel's walls. We expect each of Regent Taipei's profit centers to aspire to be the optimal choice, surpassing their counterparts in the field. A five-star hotel cannot compromise its standards in the pursuit of cost-cutting measures. The aim is not only to meet expectations but to exceed them, outperforming competitors at every turn. For sellers, it becomes imperative to consider how to deliver the desired quality within the allocated budget and to provide better value for money than outside competitors in the same price range.

The notion of fair settling of accounts is also important. For instance, we employ long-term transfer pricing strategies for room promotions that include complimentary breakfast. When dividing the expenses between the guest rooms and the Brasserie—which offers breakfast—we also take account of the fact that the guest room department drives customers to the buffet. While ensuring that operational costs remain unaffected, we coordinate a reasonable transfer price that can be lower than the standard price, allowing us to strike a balance that offers enhanced value without compromising the hotel's overall financial performance.

Creating a Culture of Ownership

What began as a management experiment years earlier has evolved into a thriving internal ecosystem—each unit empowered to act, adapt, and innovate like a business within a business.

This culture of ownership is best embodied by our external catering team. Their extensive experience in successfully executing countless events of diverse sizes and themes makes them stand out in the realm of five-star hotels, and they are often the preferred banquet team for renowned luxury brands, such as Chanel and Hermès.

The realm of high-end events encompasses myriad departments, including banquet operations, the executive chef's office, housekeeping, F&B, procurement, finance, creative arts, and flower arrangement. This internal ecosystem enables the small bosses of each department to collaborate with both internal and external partners, engage in cross-departmental innovation, and seamlessly execute a wide range of large-scale projects.

In the past, our colleagues worked under the shelter of a big tree. The establishment of the profit center system created a culture of ownership in which department heads were transformed into small bosses who were empowered to take responsibility for their work. This newfound sense of ownership enabled them to solve minor problems independently.

Taking on the mindset of a small boss has led to increased employee engagement. For those who embrace this mentality, work becomes not just a responsibility but a platform for showcasing their ability to tackle challenges rather than waiting for instructions from above. A prime example is the F&B retail division's annual mooncake promotions during the Mid-Autumn Festival. In order to leap ahead of the stiff competition in this sector to meet its sales goals, the F&B retail division has branched out to television shopping networks, department stores, and other venues to ensure the widest public awareness of its superior products.

The SARS outbreak tested the decentralized profit center system we'd established for the first time in crisis conditions—and proved it a decisive advantage. Our empowered department heads moved quickly to launch catering, deep cleaning, and other services that helped us weather the storm.

Even in routine operational circumstances, the profit center system encouraged the expansion of dining options within the hotel. For example, Regent Taipei's Brasserie originally didn't have afternoon tea service, but after the profit center system was introduced, the hotel's small bosses began thinking of ways to increase revenue by improving operational efficiency and extending business hours. After Regent Taipei began offering buffet-style afternoon tea, other hotels followed suit by serving afternoon tea at their buffet restaurants.

Once afternoon tea had been added to its breakfast, lunch, and dinner lineup, the Brasserie proposed a late-night supper club, extending its service from morning until deep into the night. This won the Brasserie such a loyal following that it became the only buffet in Taipei recommended as must-eat dining by CNN.

In the past, the best restaurants were found in five-star hotels, but independent restaurants have now gained ascendancy. We got a jump on this trend twenty years ago when we observed that many overseas hotel restaurants lost their competitive edge and eventually served only their own guests. The profit center system injected Regent Taipei restaurants with a spirit of independence and competitiveness, as drawing up their own financial reports allowed them to compare themselves directly with counterparts outside of the hotel.

It is this strategic mindset that sets Regent Taipei apart from other international hotels. Most international hotels offer at most two or three restaurants to local customers, but Regent Taipei considers F&B a core business rather than an afterthought.

The hotel boasts eight self-operated restaurants, including the Brasserie, our award-winning international buffet featuring daily-catch seafood, and Azie, an exciting fusion of Asian and Western flavors, on the first floor; the Gallery Lounge, premium steakhouse Robin's Grill, and a French-style teppanyaki restaurant, Robin's Teppanyaki, on the second floor; exquisite Cantonese cuisine at Silks House on the third floor; Shanghai and Sichuan cuisine at Lan Ting on the twenty-first floor; and Mihan Honke, offering Japanese-style hot pot shabu-shabu and sukiyaki at B3. In addition to these self-operated restaurants, the hotel collaborates with renowned chefs and restaurants to set up shop in the Regent Galleria on levels B1 and B2.

Our aim is to be the market leader in the local dining scene. It is by earning the trust and loyalty of discerning local customers that Regent Taipei attracts international travelers. It's the same process as when a traveler arrives in a foreign city and asks local connections to recommend their favorite restaurants. We strive to be the go-to dining destination, offering exceptional experiences that leave a lasting impression.

The SARS Response: Empathy in Action

The SARS pandemic inspired the executive team at Regent Taipei to free their imaginations to develop a proactive strategy to mitigate loss and ride out the crisis. Meeting the new demand for companies to stagger their employees' work locations and minimize face-to-face contact, Regent Taipei's guest rooms were reconfigured into mobile offices on month-to-month leases.

To further adapt, Regent Taipei redeployed its cleaning staff and equipment to offer top-to-bottom deep-cleaning services to homeowners in the greater Taipei area. Our F&B department also pivoted to focus on five-star banquet catering and gourmet meal home delivery services. These rapid and effective adaptations allowed Regent Taipei to not only survive the worst year of the SARS pandemic but also become the only major Asian listed hotel company to post a profit in 2003.

After the SARS pandemic, Regent Taipei continued to expand and refine its outreach efforts. In 2005, we launched our first dedicated off-site F&B services department. This new venture featured a wide variety of cuisines—from the Japanese buffet at Wasabi to the Thai-inspired Spice Market and the elegant banquet offerings of Garden Villa, which quickly became a favorite for weddings. Each concept reflected our commitment to quality and innovation while reaching customers beyond the hotel's walls.

In 2006, we took a bold step by acquiring the Domino's Pizza master franchises in Taiwan and China, building out a network of hundreds of delivery units. Two years later, we opened Silks Palace at the National Palace Museum, where culinary creativity met cultural storytelling. Its menu, inspired by classical Chinese traditions, gave guests from around the world a deeper taste of Taiwan's heritage. These ventures also became invaluable training grounds—not just for chefs and service teams but also for future hotel GMs, who honed their leadership skills there through hands-on experience.

This multifaceted approach to hotel management during the SARS period was rooted in the concept of empathy. When our clients could not come to us, we reached out to meet them where they were. It pushed our competitive strength beyond the Regent Taipei location to extend our services into the wider environment. During this phase, empathy became the core value of SHG and the guiding principle for all staff, activities, and entities within the group.

Looking back on this first transformation, I can see how the profit center system didn't just change our operations—it changed our entire mindset. The battles with Chairman Chen, painful as they were, taught me the importance of corporate governance and standing firm on principles. The SARS crisis showed us that true leadership means adapting quickly while never losing sight of our core values.

Most importantly, this period established empathy as our North Star. Whether we were creating internal transfer pricing that was fair to all parties, empowering our staff members to become small bosses, or pivoting our services to meet customers where they were during SARS, everything came back to treating others as we wished to be treated ourselves.

This foundation would prove invaluable as we faced even greater challenges in the years ahead. But we had learned something crucial: Crisis doesn't just test your business model—it reveals your character. And character, once forged in the fire of adversity, becomes an unshakeable asset that no market downturn can take away.

CHAPTER 3

Global Expansion

(2008–2018)

The decade from 2008 to 2018 marked Regent Taipei's second transformation into a global brand powerhouse. But it required surviving a financial tsunami at the beginning of that period before we became the first Taiwanese business to purchase an international luxury hospitality brand.

In 2007, cracks began to show in the US housing market as borrowers started defaulting on subprime mortgages. What had seemed like a booming real estate sector quickly unraveled, setting off a financial crisis that would ripple across the globe. One of the most dramatic moments came in September 2008, when Lehman Brothers—one of America's oldest and most respected investment banks—collapsed after heavy losses on mortgage-backed securities.

The fallout was swift and severe. Global stock markets plunged, credit froze, and businesses everywhere faced sudden liquidity shortages. Millions of people lost their jobs, and the world entered a deep and prolonged recession that reshaped the financial landscape for years to come.

Asia, however, was somewhat insulated from the worst effects. While the global economy struggled, many Asian markets—including Taiwan—managed to hold steady and even continue growing. Buoyed by this relative stability, we felt confident enough to move forward with plans that had been years in the making. In 2008 and 2009, we launched two new hotel brands: Silks, our cultural luxury offering, and Just Sleep, designed for younger, value-conscious travelers. Even amid global uncertainty, we believed there was room—and need—for bold thinking.

Breakaway Thinking

The idea behind the Silks brand began as a form of contingency planning. With our twenty-year licensing agreement for Regent Taipei set to expire in 2010—and the uncertainty of the brand's future after Regent was first acquired by Four Seasons and subsequently sold to the Carlson Group—we had to consider our next move. We saw three possible paths: rebrand as a Four Seasons, partner with another global luxury brand, or build something of our own. Silks was born out of that third option: a homegrown brand that could carry forward the values and quality we had worked hard to establish for Regent Taipei.

I personally selected names for both brands, drawing inspiration from history and guest expectations. The Silks brand offers a five-star cultural experience by taking its cues from the historical Silk Road—a once-thriving caravan network connecting trade and commerce between East and West. Just Sleep caters to budget and family travelers, offering convenience, comfort, and modern amenities with a sharp focus on the 3B priorities: bed, bath, and breakfast.

Despite challenges posed by the financial crisis, we remained committed to providing exceptional service experiences. Just Sleep not only met guests' basic expectations but also gave them the benefit of Regent Taipei's unique service DNA. Our practice in the SHG is to hire people who share our service mindset and then place them where they're needed so guests enjoy five-star service regardless of hotel brand. This approach has kept our Just Sleep brand consistently outperforming Taiwan's other budget hotels.

The Regent brand's fusion of Eastern and Western cultures was the fundamental element inspiring my vision for a new brand. The legendary Silk Road was emblematic of this cultural exchange, evoking the ancient Han and Tang dynasties in its testament to the continuous flow of business and trade. Isn't a hotel just a modern version of the ancient guesthouse, and a hotel operator the equivalent of the innkeeper of old? Naming a hotel after the Silk Road created the romantic vision of shuttling between ancient and modern, East and West.

Many other companies had already registered under the name Silk, so we added an *s* to create *Silks Place*. This name embodied the essence of silk and its associations with Chinese culture, while *Place* signified a luxurious yet understated venue. The spirit of the Silk Road aligned with our group's mission of bringing the best of Taiwan to the world and the best of the world to Taiwan. It is with this vision that we founded Silks, with the Chinese name *Jing Ying*, which means *elites* and shares perfect symmetry with Regent's *jing hua* characters in striving for a similar five-star rating with inherent cultural characteristics.

That same year, the government opened Taiwan's doors to mainland Chinese tourists, and we saw a new opportunity to create something truly unique—an affordable boutique hotel brand that would offer comfort and essential amenities in space-efficient design, enabling us to pass on rental cost savings to guests in expensive urban locations. Our goal was to provide smart and stylish hospitality that combined three-star prices with four-star amenities and five-star services. Aiming to create a community landmark that reflected neighborhood style and culture, we chose the name *Just Sleep*—simple and memorable, conveying our brand's unique selling point.

Believing that times of economic downturn require even greater commitment to investing in the future, we pushed ahead with opening the first hotels under our two new brands—Silks Place Yilan and Just Sleep Taipei Ximending—in 2009.

As it turned out, the challenging situation provided an opportunity to completely resolve the problems related to the expiration of the Regent licensing agreement.

Building Back Better

The 2008 subprime crisis presented challenges to everyone, but it also presented opportunities. During the global financial crisis, it became socially unacceptable in America to flaunt luxury in the face of economic calamity, and luxury hotels and lifestyles were in retreat. In 2009, the Carlson Group decided to sell its luxury portfolio, which included the Regent brand. It enlisted an investment bank to contact the world's top ten hotel groups as well as the owners of the ten Regent hotels worldwide.

My original calculations were simple: If the annual royalties paid to Four Seasons/Regent were higher than the annual interest paid to the bank for purchasing the Regent brand, then buying out the brand was a financially sound investment because we would not have to pay brand royalties. Acquiring the global Regent rights from Carlson would be a cash flow–positive arbitrage at the outset, with future upside from the brand's revival.

The amount of interest we had to pay was actually less than expected. We took out a bridge loan from Mega International Commercial Bank in the first year and then issued zero-interest convertible corporate bonds the following year. Convertible bonds had the advantage of reducing interest payments, increasing equity financing, and lowering our group's debt-to-equity ratio, but they required investors to have faith in our company's future growth.

Recognizing this once-in-a-lifetime opportunity to own the global Regent brand, I immediately reached out to Johanna Wang, president of the brand marketing and research firm JRV International and also a Regent Taipei board member, trusted friend, and one of the smartest people I know. After listening to my plan, Johanna wholeheartedly agreed that I couldn't let this chance slip through my fingers. This would immediately resolve our contract expiration dilemma in Regent Taipei and seamlessly secure our Regent brand affiliation in perpetuity.

Even though we had two new and exclusive hotel brands under active development, obtaining exclusive ownership of the Regent brand name on a global scale was crucial to fulfilling SHG's mission of bringing the best of the world to Taiwan, and bringing the best of Taiwan to the world. Acquiring the Regent brand would gain us entry into the world of highly coveted luxury brands and bring us one step closer to our goal of becoming an international hotel group.

As a listed company, however, we needed to proceed in strictest confidence because any rumors of such a major acquisition could lead to insider trading or other stock scandals punishable by law. I enlisted the help of my niece, Miyuki Pan, an MBA who worked in Regent Taipei's finance department, and hired Bill Sipple, a former VP of development at Carlson Companies, as project consultant. I also assembled a team of international attorneys—first, to prevent leaks and second, because the Taiwanese legal community had limited mergers and acquisitions experience with international hotel brands.

The deal involved buying a trademarked brand name and licensing rights, which was basically purchasing seventeen management agreements. This required analyzing thousands of pages of contract documentation and reference materials, with confidential clauses alone taking a week of back-and-forth communication around the clock with company representatives, lawyers, and team members across Asia, the United States, and Europe.

The Bidding Process

Starting in June 2009, Miyuki, Bill, and I worked tirelessly for half a year to create Regent Taipei's proposal and bid offer. Out of twenty initial bidders, Regent Taipei was one of five selected to move forward into the second round. At a series of meetings lasting a week at the Regent Berlin, the five bidders were asked to present their vision and plans for the global Regent brand. At that point, I realized we were up against global giants such as the Ritz-Carlton (later bought by Marriott International), the Mandarin Oriental Hotel Group, and Britain's InterContinental Hotels Group (IHG). After presenting our proposal in Berlin, Bill and I were thrilled to learn that Regent Taipei had been selected to move forward to the third round of bidding alongside IHG and a prospective buyer from Saudi Arabia.

This experience taught me that once a brand achieves global top-tier status, it also gains an upper hand in purchase negotiations. In the final round of bidding, Carlson Group meticulously reviewed each section of the purchase contract with both SHG and IHG, scoring each bidder's terms and conditions to determine the winning bid and the new owner of the Regent Hotels & Resorts hospitality brand.

In January 2010, when I learned that Carlson Companies had accepted our bid for Regent Taipei, I knew we had to act fast. I immediately informed our CFO, Dick Lin, that we were about to take on an international acquisition with high stakes and a tight timeline. The purchase agreement gave us just three months to raise the necessary funds, complete due diligence, and refile trademark registrations—a daunting checklist by any measure.

One of the biggest challenges was updating nearly four hundred separate instances of the Regent trademark across ninety-eight countries, each with its own legal and regulatory requirements. To meet the deadline, our small team worked around the clock, often coordinating across multiple time zones. Fortunately, our longstanding relationship with Mega Bank proved invaluable. Their trust in our vision and track record made the financing possible. More than a financial transaction, it was a partnership built on mutual respect—a direct result of our philosophy: Treat others as we would like to be treated, and always look for win–win outcomes.

Securing the Brand

SHG completed its acquisition of the global Regent Hotels & Resorts luxury business in June 2010, after paying Carlson Companies US$56 million (equal to around NT$1.75 billion at the time). With ownership of management contracts for seventeen existing and planned Regent properties in Europe, Asia, the Americas, and the Middle East, Regent Taipei now enjoyed a prestigious presence in key business and travel destinations—such as Beijing, Singapore, Phuket, and Bali in Asia; Berlin, Zagreb, and Bordeaux in Europe; Puerto Rico in North America; the Turks and Caicos Islands; and Abu Dhabi and Doha in the Middle East.

The Regent brand also extended its reach from land properties to the sea with the world-renowned Regent Seven Seas Cruises (RSSC) line. The midsize luxury cruise ships in RSSC's fleet provided a six-star experience with unparalleled attention to detail and service. In 2013, Regent sold its right of use of the Regent name in the cruise sector to Norwegian Cruise Line for a onetime royalty payment of NT$60 million.

Looking back, I think what tipped the scales in our favor wasn't just the numbers or the bid itself—it was empathy. We genuinely cared about the Regent brand, and I believe Carlson's team could feel that. We convinced Carlson Company executives that the Regent brand was in our bloodline and that Regent Taipei's consistent profitability and exemplary management made it the ideal company to carry the prestigious Regent brand name forward in the global market. We emphasized that Regent Taipei would cherish the Regent brand as its crown jewel rather than treat it as just another brand under a huge conglomerate and would therefore protect the value of the brand as its top priority. In short, given the narrow differences in material terms of rival bids, we secured the deal by envisioning Carlson Companies as "mother of the bride," determined to select the suitor most likely to provide a secure future to the Regent brand.

With the acquisition complete, we became the first hotel group in Taiwan to own an international luxury brand outright—a milestone that marked both a turning point and a statement of intent. What began as a management partnership had evolved step-by-step: from owner to franchisee to brand holder. Each phase brought new lessons and responsibilities, preparing us for the moment when we could shape not just a property but a brand itself. Owning Regent opened the door to building our own brands and set the foundation for the broader vision we would pursue in the years ahead.

The Regent DNA

The process of acquiring the global Regent brand gave me an opportunity to reflect on the philosophy behind what made the brand truly special. I wrote down what I called the Regent's essence, a set of twelve key concepts that I believed defined the brand's identity. Each concept consists of two different or even opposite elements that complement each other, much like yin and yang in the tai chi symbol. Although the pairings may appear polar and abstract, they actually converge to depict the duality of the brand DNA of SHG.

Imagine having to be global yet local, quiet yet confident. It sounds impossible, but the word *yet* implies possessing both qualities. While confidence is typically an external manifestation, we prefer a quiet and confident glow. Likewise, as a global brand, Regent needs to stay grounded—connected to and integrated with local culture, becoming a site of organic creation. It's like reaching for the sky while staying rooted in the ground.

Your environment doesn't decide your success or failure but gives you an opportunity to discern your true character and realize change. (photo taken at Silks Place Taroko)

This harmony of opposites approach helps avoid polarized thinking that puts things in either/or categories. We need to find ways to bring tradition and innovation together for the best possible outcome. Most important is allowing all our group's brands to tell great stories, find common ground, and showcase the essence of SHG.

The Regent DNA illustrates our mission, which is also our brand's commitment to bring the best of the world to wherever we are and the best of wherever we are to the world. We do this by rediscovering, refining, and reinterpreting in a way that is global yet local, simple yet elegant, and cultured yet innovative. We also ensure that our guests feel relaxed in a luxurious yet understated atmosphere.

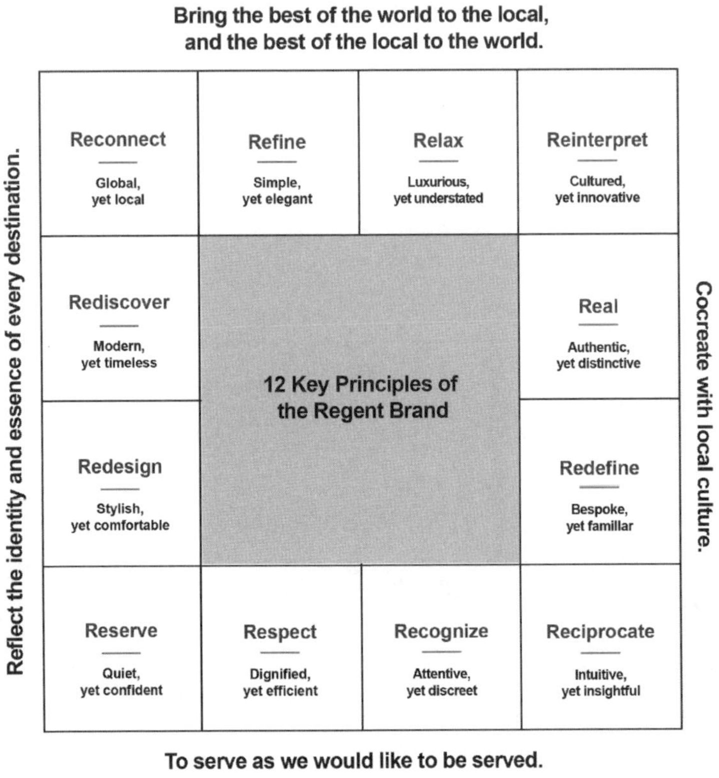

In the Regent DNA, twelve core dualities come together to define our mission and concepts on empathetic hospitality, cultural integration, and elegant design.

When we had only Regent Taipei, we focused on bringing the best of the world to Taiwan and the best of Taiwan to the world. After launching our Silks Place and Just Sleep brands, our mission became more diverse, yet still unified. Silks Place is oriented toward major city and resort destinations, so it aims to bring the best of the world to its destinations and vice versa. Just Sleep is all about local cultures, so our hotels want to showcase the best of their surrounding communities.

For each hotel we've established—whether it's the cultural luxury hotel Silks Place, local boutique hotel Just Sleep, hot-spring resort Wellspring by Silks, or our lifestyle brand SILKS X—we always ask ourselves how this hotel can connect the global to the local, refine a sense of simple yet elegant experience, and reimagine a cultured yet innovative ambiance.

Global Strategy: Sometimes Two Are Better than One

As soon as we completed our purchase of Regent Hotels & Resorts, we established its global headquarters in Taipei and refined the group's blueprint for future brand growth. The result was the creation of a brand pyramid: Regent at the peak as the international five-star luxury brand, Silks in the middle as the culturally infused regional five-star offering, and Just Sleep at the base as a stylish boutique hotel brand. With clearly defined layers, the pyramid allowed us to meet the expectations of elite, high-end, and budget travelers alike. What unified all three brands was a commitment to blending global and local elements with modern and timeless aesthetics to deliver bespoke hospitality experiences.

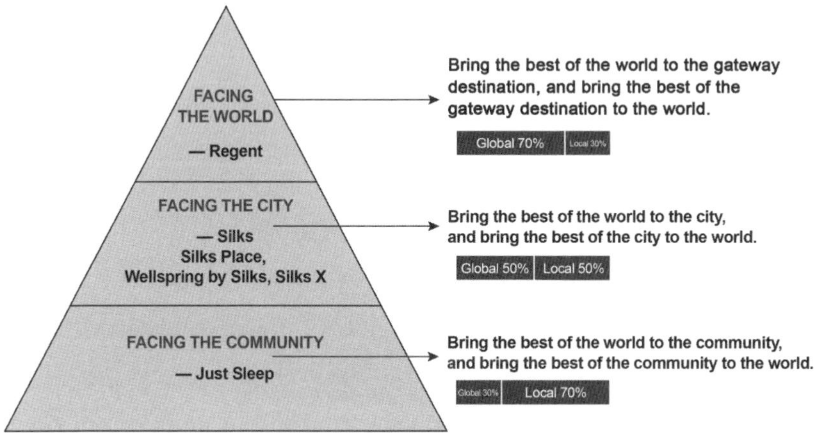

Silks Hotel Group brand pyramid

Even with a world-class international team beside me, some conversations could only happen one way: owner to owner. Regent properties were held by some of the wealthiest individuals and families on the planet—the Rothschilds and Arnaults, the Kwees of Singapore, and Madame Chan in Beijing. These were people who expected and deserved direct engagement, which meant I spent years traveling from country to country, investing time in building and deepening relationships with some of the most influential figures in global business.

Many of those encounters were fascinating and even enjoyable—these were people who lived at the highest levels of taste, expectation, and ambition. But the nonstop travel eventually caught up with me. After eight years of jet lag, late-night calls, and too little rest, I began to feel the toll it was taking on both my health and my personal life. At that point, I knew that managing and expanding a global brand couldn't rely on nonstop travel alone.

As we began shaping Regent into a true global brand, several major challenges quickly came into focus. The first was financial: Building and maintaining an international network came with enormous costs. To support even one regional center on each continent, we would need at least ten active hotels in each region. But coming out of the global financial crisis, the industry was headed in the opposite direction. New development had slowed, and many groups were scaling back. Given that reality, there was a strong case to focus our efforts on Asia—where we already had momentum—rather than stretch ourselves too thin pursuing an international footprint in the Americas, Europe, and the Middle East.

The second hurdle was the costly lease we had to inherit for Regent Berlin. Despite being a fine hotel with solid revenue, Regent Berlin was burdened with onerous building rental that brought annual net losses of around €2 million, offsetting the profitability of other Regent properties.

Finally, Regent's reliance on dispatching Asia-based staff around the world rather than developing regional management infrastructure was hindering the company's efforts to implement network-wide brand and operational initiatives.

After nearly eight years of shouldering Regent's brand-building mission, I saw an opportunity in 2018 to forge a strategic alliance with IHG, which had been our rival in the last phase of bidding for the Regent brand. Trading on both the London and the New York stock exchanges, IHG owns around a dozen renowned hotel brands worldwide, including InterContinental Hotels & Resorts, Kimpton Hotels & Restaurants, Hotel Indigo, Crowne Plaza, and Holiday Inn.

IHG acquired a 51 percent share in the Regent brand and took over the lease of Regent Berlin as well as the expansion and operation of Regent hotels worldwide. This move allowed our Taiwan headquarters to focus on Regent brand activities in Taiwan. Most importantly, the joint venture allowed for the rebranding of InterContinental Hong Kong back to Regent Hong Kong in 2023—a dream come true.

This new strategy for developing the global brand benefited both partners. IHG finally owned a luxury brand that could compete with the likes of Four Seasons and the Ritz-Carlton. The move also connected Regent Taipei to IHG's operating platform, giving it access to IHG's global guest loyalty reservation system.

The advantages of this alliance extended beyond operational efficiency. SHG was able to leverage the economies of scale from IHG's more than six thousand hotels to save on the expense of creating an exclusive back-end system for Regent's global network. This allowed SHG to focus on extending and deepening the competitive advantages of its core brands in the home market.

By selling half its shares in the Regent brand to IHG, SHG freed up the resources and energy needed to move into its next phase of development. At SHG, we could now focus our full attention on developing the unique value and position of the SHG hotel brands—Regent, Silks, Wellspring, and Just Sleep—while also developing new luxury living and mixed-use projects in Taiwan inspired by the five-star "mixed-use lifestyle platform" demonstrated by Regent Porto Montenegro and Regent Phu Quoc.

I like to say that fate put the Regent brand in our hands twenty years after Regent Taipei opened in 1990. Staying loyal to Regent was a huge gain in the long run, although that wasn't always apparent at the time. Our joint venture with IHG was only possible because of our loyalty to the Regent brand despite the rebranding of Regent hotels under Four Seasons ownership. By 2009, our Regent Taipei, Regent Singapore, and Regent Beverly Wilshire were the only original Regents left. By being in the right place at the right time, we took on stewardship of the Regent name and the mission of reviving it to its former glory.

The Regent Beverly Wilshire opened in 1990, sharing the same inaugural year as Regent Taipei. Its exposure as the key location in the movie Pretty Woman, *starring Julia Roberts and Richard Gere, gained it widespread popularity and helped establish Regent's brand image as a favorite among international superstars.*

Turning Crisis into Opportunity

How has SHG maintained its innovative mindset even during economic downturns? Transforming our circumstances requires perceiving the yin-yang relationship between opportunity and adversity and focusing on that critical point where one becomes the other. Under certain circumstances, misfortune can lead to a positive outcome and serve as prerequisite to good fortune.

The 2008 global financial crisis was not only devastating to hotel revenue streams but also made construction of new hotels impossible because banks were unwilling to issue construction loans. The solution we came up with to address the lack of hotel financing was to develop a business model that combined hotels with residences for a new kind of luxury living experience. The sale of hotel-branded residences returned at least half—if not most—of the total investment capital for the owner-developer while bringing in sustained revenue streams in the form of royalties and fees from hotel management services. In other words, we met our hotel capital shortfall by using the proceeds from the sale of luxury residential premises as a substitute for bank loans.

One of our earliest examples of this strategy in action was Regent's entry into Porto Montenegro—a coastal harbor known for its rugged beauty, often compared to Monte Carlo. Once the largest naval base in the former Yugoslavia, the area was transformed after being acquired by a consortium of ultra-high-net-worth families, including Peter Munk, the Rothschilds, and the Arnaults. Its rise was further boosted by a destination cameo in the 2006 James Bond film *Casino Royale*, which gave it global visibility.

The project began when Regent President Ralf Ohletz joined a panel on mixed-use development at the Marche International des Professionnels de I'Immobilier real estate forum held in Europe after the financial crisis. Seated next to the owner of the Porto Montenegro property, Ralf spoke about the future of branded hotel residences within the context of mixed-use hospitality. Coincidentally, the owner was articulating his vision of remaking Porto Montenegro into Monte Carlo, a multiphase mixed-use development combining marinas, the yacht industry, casinos, entertainment, retail, and residences. The conversation struck a chord. The owner, who had been in negotiations with Four Seasons for two years without reaching an agreement, was impressed by our shared vision and openness to innovation.

The grand opening ceremony of Regent Porto Montenegro took place in 2014. From left to right: Prime Minister of Montenegro Milo Đukanović, Barrick Gold Mining's founder Peter Munk, Steven Pan, and Lord Rothschild.

That moment of alignment turned into momentum. We began negotiating a hotel management and residential licensing contract in the midst of the financial crisis. The owner's Managing Director Oliver Corlette later came to Taiwan to finalize the deal—and to explore Taiwan's emerging yacht industry. When the Regent Hotel and Residences officially opened in 2014, it marked two industry firsts: the first new luxury hotel to open in Europe after the global financial crisis and the debut of hotel-branded residences on the continent. Regent helped pioneer the mixed-use hospitality model in Europe by turning the disruption of 2008 into a platform for reinvention.

I remember a conversation I had with one of our owner-partners at the Regent Montenegro superyacht marina as he was having his yacht refueled. He asked me to guess how much it cost to gas up the yacht. I threw out what I thought was an enormous sum of $50,000, but he gave a thumbs-up gesture, indicating that it was even higher. I guessed $100,000, and his thumb went up again. Finally, he told me it took a quarter of a million US dollars to gas up his yacht for a single outing! He had a crew of fifteen on his yacht, about the same as a small boutique hotel.

Frankly, I was also curious about why a superyacht marina even needed a hotel, since people can just live on their yachts. I learned that the hotel provides housing for yacht crews between trips and also offers respite for guests of yacht owners, who sometimes need a break from seaborne life and from the lifestyles of their hosts.

Regent has further developed the hotel-residence business model to become the world's leading brand in hotel-residence properties, with successful ventures in Jakarta, Indonesia, and Phu Quoc, Vietnam—and a residence-only venture in Boston. Average property values at Regent hotel-residences have regularly outperformed other luxury branded hotel-residences, and with each new development phase selling out quickly, we were well into phase 4 of residences when the Investment Corporation of Dubai acquired the entire Porto Montenegro project in 2016.

The rapid financial growth of SHG was naturally reflected in its share price, emerging as the top-performing stock in Taiwan around 2015 during notably overheated cross-strait travel hype. I reminded my colleagues that prices can plummet as easily as they can rise—as we had seen after the 9/11 terrorist attacks, when Regent Taipei's share price crashed to penny stock status. The ability to maintain positive earnings momentum is the only way to ensure genuine long-term sustainability and growth.

Regent pioneered a fresh business model spearheaded by its flagship project, Regent Porto Montenegro in the Republic of Montenegro. This development marked a significant milestone as the first integrated complex in Europe that seamlessly blends a hotel with luxury residential properties.

At Regent Taipei, I've always placed a strong emphasis on consistent performance—not just in terms of operations but also regarding delivering consistent EPS growth and returning maximum dividends to reward the commitment of our long-term investors and employees. From the beginning, our goal has been to build an enterprise that can stand the test of time. That means preparing for future headwinds, especially during the best of times. When challenges do come—as they always do—we draw on that preparation and resilience to turn setbacks into opportunities. That mindset, more than any short-term share price, is what defines sustainable success.

A Pandemic Success: Five-Star Hotel and Residential Development

In early May 2022, Regent Phu Quoc, located on Vietnam's largest island, opened for business. The grand unveiling marked the debut of Asia's most triumphant five-star resort and villa project, a masterpiece whose sales more than doubled the total development cost. This was a remarkable achievement in that villas were sold out during the pandemic and upon the hotel's grand opening.

Regent Phu Quoc enjoys a wealth of breathtaking natural beauty, nestled alongside a UNESCO world biosphere reserve and graced by pristine white sand beaches. We carved out two lagoons to harness the full splendor of the environment and ensure that every villa on site enjoys sea views. The complex comprises 120 hotel rooms, 42 two-bedroom Sky Villas, and 80 two- to four-bedroom Land Villas, for a grand total of 420 keys. Each Sky Villa has its own private pool with panoramic ocean views, and every Land Villa has multiple pools with each bedroom having its own private pool—for a grand total of 252 pools!

The question of optimal value creation looms large. The secret behind the resounding success of this integrated development project is the transformation of real estate into a dual-purpose financial instrument—both a personal haven and an investment capable of generating steady cash flow. Purchasers of the villas become landlords who entrust the hotel with overseeing their property. During periods of non-occupancy by owners, the villas are seamlessly pooled into the broader resort room mix and become sources of income for their owners. For example, a two-bedroom Sky Villa can be booked as a complete unit or partitioned into two distinct rooms (two keys), catering to the needs of families on weekends and couples on weekdays alike.

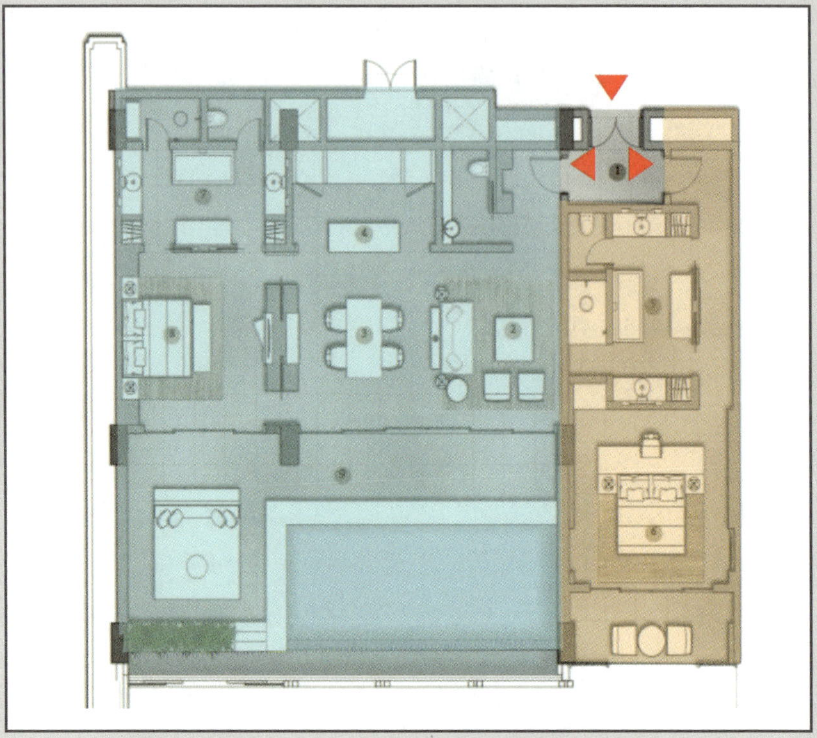

Interior floor plan of a two-bedroom Sky Villa

The concept of fusing a five-star hotel with residential living forms the cornerstone of Regent's development strategy. With Regent's sterling reputation for luxury and innovation across Asia, Europe, and the Americas, developers can be confident that they'll rapidly recoup the steep cost of land acquisition and construction. The Regent brand can accelerate unit presale and turnover and maximize cash flow, both at the front end for developers and at the back end for buyers from hotel revenue sharing.

This kind of real estate project, designed to optimize cash flow, requires the meticulous orchestration of a five-star hotel brand for its true potential to materialize. Regent is therefore not just a luxury residential brand but also an investment vehicle for reliable cash flow.

That's because we understand that a modern lifestyle encompasses not solely the joys of dining, revelry, and leisure but extends to investment and real estate. The transformation of a hotel residential complex into cash flow–producing real estate is the pivotal facet of such a lifestyle.

All of the suites and villas at the Regent Phu Quoc complex have sea views, and each Sky Villa room has a private swimming pool.

Opened in early May 2022, Regent Phu Quoc unveiled its splendor on Vietnam's largest island, fronted by a pristine beach and alongside an UNESCO-designated world biosphere reserve.

Regent Jakarta sets a new standard in luxury residences.

Boston's Echelon Seaport Towers by Regent—Echelon Seaport Towers collaborates with Regent to set a new luxury benchmark in Boston.

Regent Residences, the five-star luxury home brand, is found on three continents—Europe, Asia, and North America—and is becoming Regent's primary development model (top image: Regent Porto Montenegro in Tivat, Montenegro; bottom image: Regent Phu Quoc on Phu Quoc Island, Vietnam).

Aiming for a Triple Win

After nearly eight years of building the Regent brand independently, we had reached a crossroads. The brand had gained global visibility, but maintaining that momentum across continents required infrastructure beyond our scale. That's when an unexpected opportunity emerged: a strategic alliance with our one-time rival, IHG. It began, like many pivotal business deals, with a conversation.

Over the years, three successive IHG CEOs approached me about acquiring the Regent brand outright. But to me, buying the Regent brand wasn't just a matter of cashing out; my goal was long-term development and, if possible, to bring Regent Hong Kong back to life.

On June 30, 2009, just after we'd completed the Regent acquisition, IHG's CEO Andy Cosslett arranged for me to meet with him at the InterContinental Hong Kong. When he learned that I wouldn't consider selling the Regent brand outright, he suggested a cooperative arrangement that would allow Regent Taipei to develop extensions of the Regent brand under the IHG umbrella, but I declined the proposal.

The next IHG CEO, Richard Solomons—an experienced former CFO—sent over a fixed-price offer to buy the Regent brand every year, reflecting both his persistence and his focus on current asset valuations. The hotel industry is known for its cordial competition, and Richard's steady check-ins eventually developed into a genuine friendship.

IHG's third CEO, Keith Barr, took the helm in 2016. Having previously served as IHG's president for Greater China, he not only appreciated the historical significance of Regent Hong Kong but also recognized the immense brand value that could be gained from restoring the Regent name to the InterContinental Hong Kong.

Working closely with our consultant Eric Levy, we spent a full year crafting a joint venture framework consisting of five separate agreements covering share purchase terms, joint venture governance, management and development rights, trademarks, and the permanent carve-out of Regent Taiwan. The joint venture arrangement included put and call share options to ensure the alignment of interests between the two hotel groups.

Once the framework was in place, our board approved the sale of 51 percent of Regent Hotels & Resorts to IHG, effectively giving them controlling interest and decision-making power related to the Regent brand. Despite IHG taking over Regent development and management operations globally, SHG retained 100 percent control over Regent Taipei and all future rights of Regent in Taiwan. Additionally, the agreement included a repurchase clause to ensure that IHG would meet all obligations and actively develop and expand the Regent brand. Failure to meet obligations would result in IHG paying a price equal to three times the original purchase cost. The agreement allowed Regent to flourish under IHG's global reach while aligning the interests of both parties.

It might look as if I'd relinquished control over the Regent brand, but in actuality, we'd put together an arrangement whereby Regent Taipei, IHG, and Goodwin Gaw all came out better than before—a perfect three-way win.

The first win was Goodwin Gaw's ability to proudly restore the Regent name to his newly acquired property. In 2015, IHG expressed interest in selling InterContinental Hong Kong, but the deal-breaker for me was that the hotel would have to be managed and named by the InterContinental brand for the next fifty years. This was a significant setback. After buying the Regent brand, we desperately needed a flagship property in a gateway city such as New York, Hong Kong, or London, and we had not yet found a suitable location.

As luck would have it, InterContinental Hong Kong was sold in 2015 to Gaw Capital Partners for a staggering US$1 billion. The founder, Goodwin Gaw, is an old friend of mine, and as a Hong Kong native, he recognized the significance of Regent Hong Kong as a symbol of Hong Kong's modern heritage. Soon after that, I encountered Goodwin at a Forbes Leadership Conference in Manila, where we had both been invited as speakers. We talked about the once-in-a-lifetime chance to restore the fifty-year-old hotel to its former glory. But the original problem remained: We were still bound to the InterContinental name for another fifty years, frustrating our determination to see the Regent Hong Kong name once again shine in Victoria Harbor.

"Would you be willing to work with IHG?" Goodwin asked me.

"Apart from selling out completely," I replied, "I'd be willing to discuss anything."

The second win was IHG's ability to fill the gap in its luxury hotel offering and compete at a higher level with other global hotel groups, such as Marriott's Ritz-Carlton, Hilton's Waldorf Astoria, and Four Seasons. IHG could also leverage the rebranding of InterContinental Hong Kong to showcase Regent Hong Kong as the new luxury flagship property and catapult Regent's global reputation and future prospects. With almost six thousand hotel locations worldwide, IHG could invest in expanding Regent's ten global properties to fifty or more over the next decade, bringing profitability in both the short and long term.

The third win was the realization of my own dream to bring back Regent Hong Kong. In addition, IHG's purchase of the insolvent Regent Berlin ended our costly lease payments on that property, which had negatively impacted our EPS. IHG's extensive global network would be able to manage the Regent portfolio much better than I could alone and more rapidly expand Regent's presence on the international stage, and I could enjoy a modicum of work–life balance.

Letting go of control helped me understand Laozi's principle of purposeful inaction. By stepping back, I watched our partner take the lead in developing Regent's global network—while we continued to share in its future growth and enjoyed the immense scale and coverage of IHG.

The Hidden Price of Growth

While adversity often creates new opportunities, it's important to recognize the reverse: Success can breed the seeds of its own downfall. Human nature tends to settle into comfort during periods of prosperity, which is precisely when discipline and foresight are most needed to prepare for harder times ahead.

My own experience acquiring the global Regent brand is a case in point. While the deal brought our hotel group a major breakthrough, it also introduced complications we hadn't fully anticipated. It taught me a valuable lesson: Success comes with hidden costs—often paid in time, energy, and the quiet toll on our mental and physical well-being.

When we acquired the Regent brand in 2010, the purchase included seventeen licensed hotel management contracts around the world, as well as licensing rights to the RSSC line. After the deal closed, I shared the following message with our Regent Taipei staff:

> Dear Colleagues,
>
> I am pleased to share with you now a piece of truly exciting news! With this afternoon's approval from the Board of Directors, Regent Taipei will be concluding the final details necessary to purchase the exclusive rights to the worldwide Regent Hotels & Resorts hospitality brand. Once completed, Regent Taipei will become the first company in Taiwan's tourism sector to own a world-class international hotel brand.
>
> This is a "homecoming" for me worthy of celebration. When Regent Taipei first opened its doors twenty years ago, we took great care to weave many of Regent's best traits into our innovative philosophy of business. Now, twenty years on, we are blessed with a tightly knit organization that has worked as one to see Regent Taipei successfully surmount multiple challenges while remaining consistently dedicated to the singular goal of delivering world-class, 5-star service to each and every guest. Regent Taipei is naturally the best company in the world to shepherd the regenerative transformation of the Regent brand through the coming decades, and

best prepared to invest in the Regent brand with the spirit and character necessary for long-term, sustainable growth.

Our ability to assume control of the global Regent operation reflects brilliantly on the twenty years of effort we all have invested in creating today's sustainable and reliable Regent Taipei organization. It also means that the world sees and recognizes the fruit of Regent Taipei's efforts. Over the next twenty years, we will take our place on the global stage and reinvigorate Regent into the world's most respected luxury hotel brand. I look forward to facing this exciting challenge with all of you!

-Steven Pan

Reading this letter now brings back memories of that heady moment when we were making headlines as the first Taiwanese business to own a world-renowned luxury hotel brand. The acquisition allowed us to stop paying licensing fees and gave us full control over how the brand would grow and evolve. Hotel owners from around the world reached out to discuss joining the brand. In the language of my father's shipping industry, Regent Taipei had gone from being a *port of call* to becoming the *home port* of the Regent name.

With the brand securely under our stewardship, I reached out to Regent founder Robert H. Burns and invited him to return as honorary chairman—a nod to the brand's roots. Robert, a legendary figure in hospitality, launched Regent in 1970 and was later joined by partners Adrian Zecha and Georg Rafael. Together, they expanded Regent to seventeen hotels worldwide including the iconic Regent Hong Kong and Regent Beverley Wilshire. Four Seasons acquired the Regent chain in 1992 and established itself as the leading global luxury brand by converting Regent properties that were under development in New York (designed by I. M. Pei), Bali, Milan, and Istanbul to the

Four Seasons brand. Moreover, Regent Hotels in Bangkok, Chiang Mai, Jakarta, and Sydney were also absorbed into the Four Seasons chain. In 1998, Carlson Group acquired the Regent name for new hotel developments while Four Seasons continued to manage existing Regent hotels such as Regent Beverley Wilshire and Singapore.

Before accepting my invitation, Robert expressed a desire to return to Regent Taipei for a visit. I was confident he would come on board. After all, much of our planning and design at Regent Taipei had been inspired by his iconic flagship: Regent Hong Kong.

Although the first Regent opened in Hawaii, it was in Hong Kong that the brand truly found its voice. The hotel's debut in 1981 ushered in a golden era—earning international acclaim and becoming a benchmark for luxury travel. Over time, the hotel won dozens of prestigious awards—including Condé Nast's best hotel in the world for many years—and cemented Regent's reputation as one of the finest names in hospitality. It was a legend of Hong Kong and shared memories of our generation. But the 1999 Asian financial crisis dealt a major blow to its owner, New World Development, which sold the property to IHG in 2000. Renamed InterContinental Hong Kong, the hotel became IHG's crown jewel in Asia and helped propel its expansion into the region's luxury markets over the next two decades.

We hoped that acquiring the Regent brand might someday allow us to restore its most iconic property—Regent Hong Kong. At the time, we didn't know that this dream would eventually involve an unexpected turn with our former rival, IHG.

In the years that followed, our wish came full circle. When Regent Hong Kong reopened in 2023, it fulfilled a dream I had carried for over a decade. Restoring the Regent name to its iconic harbor-front location was more than a business milestone—it was a personal and professional homecoming. IHG's global reach made the revival possible, while our joint venture ensured we retained control of Regent in Taiwan. With stunning views of Victoria Harbor and a design that honors the hotel's original spirit, the new Regent Hong Kong reclaimed its place as the crown jewel of the brand. For me, seeing the Regent flag flying again in the city where the brand found its voice was worth every compromise we made to get there and was a testament to my stewardship of the brand.

Embracing Duality in Life

Most people are aware of change when it happens.

The difference is in people's attitude and reaction to change.

This mindset and reaction will determine whether change becomes a crisis or an opportunity.

The ancient Greeks engraved the maxim "know thyself" at the entrance to Apollo's temple at Delphi as a timeless reminder of the crucial life mission of self-discovery.

In the context of entrepreneurship and modern life, another maxim might better serve as a guiding principle: "Recognize the coexistence of blessing with adversity." Throughout my years at Regent Taipei and SHG, I have found that a keen awareness of how adversity and advantage are two sides of the same coin has guided me through the myriad challenges and opportunities that arise in the business world.

Every entrepreneur has a fundamental principle guiding his or her journey. In my case, I have found solace in the philosophical perspective of the *Tao Te Ching*, a work traditionally attributed to the ancient Chinese philosopher Laozi in the fifth century BCE. Its perspective has lighted my way through the darkest episodes of my life and career, beginning with my hard battle with Tuntex to protect minority shareholder rights, and continuing throughout a series of macroeconomic calamities, including 9/11 and the SARS epidemic.

The opening of Regent Hong Kong in 1981 marked Regent's rise into the ranks of the world's top luxury hotel brands. Regent Hong Kong was named the world's best hotel for ten consecutive years, and the Regent name has become indelibly associated with luxury hotel services.

The Regent Taipei building, designed by the architects C. Y. Lee and Partners and with interior design by Chhada Siembieda & Associates (who also designed the Hong Kong Regent), seamlessly blends modern architectural elements with a timeless traditional lattice symbol, showcasing the hotel's unique fusion of Eastern simplicity and Western elegance.

My introduction to Laozi's teachings came in the form of a book given to me by Professor Ma Yi-kung while I was undergoing the extremely stressful challenge of parting ways with Chen Yu-Hao and Tuntex in 1999. The book was *The Serious Side of Laozi: AI Musings on the* Tao Te Ching by Chu Bong-foo. It was an ancient text reinterpreted by a modern AI expert by deconstructing each of the 5,000 Chinese characters in the book to discern its original meanings. I read it cover-to-cover multiple times and discovered an entirely new approach to life that helped me shift my mindset and gain a new perspective over the myriad problems I was facing.

During that costly battle for control of Regent Taipei, I was plagued with uncertainty and even began to question my own decisions. The burden of responsibility weighed heavily on my shoulders, and my exhaustion and mental torment caused such severe hair loss that by my early thirties I looked like a much older man who had seen and experienced too much. Laozi's philosophy became a balm for my soul, as well as a framework for facing life's uncertainties that surpassed anything I had previously encountered. I learned the importance of purposeful inaction (*wu-wei*), as well as the capacity for flexibility and tempering discord to achieve harmony. I also came to understand that when things reach an extreme, they will move in the opposite direction, like reversion to the mean. *Tao Te Ching*'s teachings helped me become resolute, motivated by goodwill, and faithful to the right path even in the face of extreme adversity. Ultimately, it helped me fulfill the meaning of my Chinese name Sy-Lian which translates to "let there be light."

Laozi's philosophy was inspired by his profound observation of nature. Some people interpret Laozi's philosophy of *wu-wei* as being passive and "doing nothing," but I feel that it actually means to be proactive without self-interest. Nature is not passive or selfish: It generously provides air and water to every living being and never asks for anything in return. I realized that people can also live this way by acting in the best interest of an organization or society, instead of clutching every good thing to themselves. I came to understand that benefit doesn't have to be a zero-sum game, and that the happiness and wellbeing of others actually enriches my own life as well.

Over the years I have come to appreciate the duality of blessing and adversity as an objective law of the universe. As the *Tao Te Ching* suggests, adversity and blessing are intertwined, with good fortune waiting in the wings of disaster and disaster lurking in the shadow of good fortune. Thus, it is impossible to know whether a situation is a disaster or a stroke of good fortune until it has played out to the end. The key to changing one's circumstances is recognizing the mutuality that binds adversity and blessing.

Many believe that change is the norm and beyond our control. But is that the only way to see things? It is true that change is all around us, and a crisis (that is, something we're not prepared for) can erupt at any moment. In my observation, most people are capable of sensing change; it is their approach and response to change that determines whether it will turn into a crisis or an opportunity. We see this played out time and time again in real life.

I have learned to appreciate life more fully by embracing cycles and the changes they bring rather than clinging to an impossible status quo. These cycles are similar to the four seasons. In the springtime of life, we grow to maturity and embark on studies and learning. In summer we start our careers and raise families to thrive and gain experience in action. In the autumn we harvest the wisdom and rewards we have gained and share it with family, friends, and the world. Then winter comes, and we can relax and enjoy the rewards of our hard efforts as we retire and recess.

In human life, this larger cycle seldom happens more than once, but for companies, the stock-market, or a nation, a winter-like crisis that looks like impending demise can actually kick-start a new spring. The key is resilience. Each season of the year has its good and bad attributes. There are maybe two weeks in autumn when we think, "This is perfect! If only the whole year could be like this!" But in fact, many people who live in temperate climates where the weather is basically nice all the time find themselves missing the variety of the seasons and the challenging monsoons or winter chills that strengthen their constitution and endurance. Likewise, a company can gain strength and new competencies from the challenges it faces and emerge prepared to face even greater challenges in the future. Recognizing the harmony of opposites and the inextricable duality of blessing and adversity is the DNA of SHG.

Crossing from Disaster to Success

The British-American philosopher Alan Watts (1915-1973) was famous for his retelling of "The Story of the Chinese Farmer," which he attributed to Laozi's teachings. The actual origin of the story is uncertain, but it is very relevant to this book and my personal experience. This is how Watts recounted the story in one of his lectures:

> *Once upon a time there was a Chinese farmer whose horse ran away. That evening, all of his neighbors came around to commiserate. They said, "We are so sorry to hear your horse has run away. This is most unfortunate." The farmer said, "Maybe." The next day the horse came back bringing seven wild horses with it, and in the evening everybody came back and said, "Oh, isn't that lucky. What a great turn of events. You now have eight horses!" The farmer again said, "Maybe."*
>
> *The following day his son tried to break one of the horses, and while riding it, he was thrown and broke his leg. The neighbors then said, "Oh dear, that's too bad," and the farmer responded, "Maybe." The next day the conscription officers came around to conscript people into the army, and they*

> *rejected his son because he had a broken leg. Again all the neighbors came around and said, "Isn't that great!" Again, he said, "Maybe."*[2]

The whole process of nature is an integrated process of immense complexity, and it's really impossible to tell whether anything that happens in it is good or bad—because you never know what will be the consequence of the misfortune; or, you never know what will be the consequences of good fortune.

Over time, I have learned that transforming our circumstances requires perceiving the tipping point between adversity and blessing. In architecture, this kind of intermediate zone creates a harmonious balance between two separate spaces. The boundary where misfortune crosses over into blessing (or vice-versa) is like the yin-yang symbol handed down in the *Tao Te Ching*, in which the black and white areas contain a spot of the opposite color. The white half, representing Yang, the positive force, contains a black dot, and the black half, representing Yin, the negative force, contains a white dot. This symbol illustrates that the good and bad are always coupled, that misfortune can lead to fortune and vice versa, and that all things arise from this combination of negative and positive forces.

The yin-yang symbol has long been admired for its representation of mutual respect, tolerance, and interdependence. Some see it as a pair of fish nestled closely together along the median line, with eyes of opposing colors. When a small dot is placed within each eye, it signifies the old giving birth to the new. This imagery epitomizes the harmony that can exist within change, where the good and bad are invariably intertwined. Disaster can be the precursor to good fortune,

---

2 Craftdeology, "'The Story of the Chinese Farmer' by Alan Watts," last accessed July 8, 2025, https://www.craftdeology.com/the-story-of-the-chinese-farmer-by-alan-watts/.

and vice versa, depending on the circumstances. This realization completely transformed the way I approached adversity.

The yin-yang tai chi symbol captures the harmony of opposites.

What captivates me about the yin-yang symbol is the profound wisdom behind its seemingly dichotomous nature. The boundary that separates black from white and yin from yang is neither one nor the other. It is a neutral space, a blank canvas brimming with boundless potential. Just like the white spaces in an ink-wash painting or the ethereal spaces between stone and sculpted sand in Japanese rock gardens, it is those empty spaces that most capture our attention. For me, it is a reminder that even in the midst of chaos, there is always a space for creativity and new beginnings.

Since not everything gained is a blessing, and not every loss is a disaster, how are you to tell whether your current situation is one of advantage or adversity? As a bellwether of the service economy, the hotel industry is usually most impacted by macroeconomic swings and global crises. Through years of navigating its ups and downs, I've come to realize that the environment hasn't dictated success or failure, but rather has given me the opportunity to discover and cultivate my character.

We all have the ability to grow and mature, and valuable life lessons can change our mindset and create the momentum necessary for change. However, self-awareness is critical to seeing the process of change through to its conclusion. Only those who have found peace of mind persist until the end. With peace of mind, we are able to perceive that everything that happens has a meaning, and rather than let a crisis go to waste, we will grasp the opportunity for change.

Spice of Life

The greatest benefit of the IHG deal was that it allowed me to reclaim my personal time. I set myself the goal of learning something new every year. In recent years, I've learned to play the piano and even the saxophone, and I've also learned Muay Thai and book publishing. Ideally, I try to divide my working hours into four quadrants: SHG Regent, investing, learning, and wellness.

Spiritual enrichment has always been a top priority for me. After realizing the relationship between blessing and adversity, I have come to feel the importance of living in the present and especially making the most of times of crisis.

To me, a crisis is any situation that is a threat to equilibrium and where transformation is necessary to recalibrate expectations and discover new possibilities. The emotions these occasions bring about should not be neglected. I have found that music is a spice that helps adjust the flavor of the changing circumstances I need to address.

Music has always been an integral part of my life, providing a soundtrack to my days and nights. I find myself drawn to different genres depending on the moment: the smooth sounds of jazz late at night, the rhythmic beats of hip hop and rap to pump me up during my daily commute, and the energy of 1980s new wave to share with friends.

When I'm alone, my heart sings to the timeless melodies of classical music. I lose myself in the grandeur of Mahler's symphonies, the intricate piano masterpieces of Chopin, and the powerful overtures of Wagnerian opera. Just as a chef uses a blend of spices to craft a one-of-a-kind dish, I rely on music as one of the spiritual ingredients needed to create a perfectly seasoned life.

It was my older brother Roger who first introduced me to the world of contemporary Western pop music when he played the latest hits at the parties he hosted at our home and enlisted me to serve as his DJ. Although I've never gained true proficiency with an instrument myself, my love for music has only grown stronger over time.

Apart from being Regent Taipei's CEO, I'm also its head DJ—because I recognize the power of music to highlight and enhance the different latent "flavors" in the atmosphere of hotel spaces. I take special care in creating appropriate playlists for our public areas, restaurants, and special events. For our thirtieth anniversary gala in 2020, I curated a playlist featuring hit songs performed by some of the international recording stars who had graced Regent Taipei with their presence over the past three decades.

I can't imagine a world in which there would be only one kind of music. Music, like life, is made up of different moods, memories, interpretations, and emotions that enrich the human experience. It is also like managing a business in terms of the need for an expansive vision in order to perceive truth and achieve genuine connection.

My passion for music extends to my secret identity as Regent Taipei's DJ, including curating the playlist for Regent Taipei's thirtieth anniversary gala in 2020.

CHAPTER 4

The Ultimate Test

(2020–2021)

Regent Taipei's third transformation began with the global COVID-19 pandemic. As the hotel entered its thirtieth year against the bleak economic outlook of 2020, its survival was threatened by an almost complete curtailment of international travel and border closure in Taiwan.

During the SARS outbreak in 2003, Regent Taipei had introduced a color-based system to track revenue shortfalls in our financial results. Yellow indicated a 25 percent decline, and red signified a 50 percent drop. During the COVID-19 pandemic, the financial reports for both guest and restaurant services were flooded with red ink, sometimes indicating an 80 percent drop in revenues.

The SARS crisis had receded within six months, but COVID-19 was clearly more severe and far-reaching. Borders were closed, flights were grounded, and entire cities went under lockdown as governments all over the world struggled to contain the spread of the virus. It was clear that we had to prepare for a long and arduous decline before we could hope for any substantial rebound in the global hotel industry.

People are the core of the hospitality industry. Whether the accommodations are luxurious or basic, the fundamental purpose of the sector is people providing services for other people. With their customer base evaporating, many hotels immediately instituted heavy staffing cutbacks in order to survive. Employment in the US lodging sector, for example, plummeted 50 percent by May 2020. The American Hotel & Lodging Association estimated in January 2021 that the COVID-19 pandemic had wiped out ten years of job growth in the accommodations sector.

Around one hundred thousand people were employed in Taiwan's hotel industry at that time, including three thousand in SHG. As many hotels shut down and laid off staff, I assured our employees that they would retain their jobs and that their futures with the hotel group were secure. I also represented the domestic hotel industry in lobbying the government for public subsidies to support employee wages and supplementary training. Regent Taipei became the first hotel in Taiwan to institute comprehensive COVID-19 standard operating procedures, and our guidelines were eventually adopted by quarantine hotels nationwide.

Regent Hotel Academy: A Learning Culture in Action

At the beginning of the pandemic, I took on a new role within Regent Taipei—chief learning officer. If the outside world had changed overnight, our inner world needed to change too. What began as a survival tactic soon became a strategic initiative we called Regent Hotel Academy.

I rediscovered the concept of a learning organization through Peter M. Senge's *The Fifth Discipline*, a seminal book on helping people constantly evolve and enhance their creative capabilities. It has inspired in me a deep desire to create a special place where everyone can become both a mentor and a mentee. That place is Regent Hotel Academy, where different generations could share wisdom and learn from one another.

The famous Roman historian Sallustius once said, "If the soul is the source of all things, then all things evolve from the soul; if wisdom is the source, then all things will be wise; but if existence is the source, then the commonality of all things is existence itself."[3] The pandemic made me realize that our hotel group exists through a process of collective learning and creation that empowers everyone to maximize their potential. That insight shaped how I thought about leadership.

For me, a leader's most important task is to create an energy cycle within the company and ensure that the cycle is in constant motion. When energy circulates continuously, we can overcome crises and be renewed in the midst of change. My approach is to use co-learning to work with everyone to create solutions to difficult problems.

Execution and Innovation

It was during the pandemic that the government's relief subsidies and tourism-industry talent-transformation training program finally presented a unique opportunity to realize my vision for Regent Hotel Academy.

In the first year, we implemented Taiwan's first self-organized training program, requiring each employee to complete 120 hours of coursework within four months—both online and in person. I contributed by hosting weekly Regent Talk sessions with each GM, where we explored innovation, leadership, and organizational wisdom—

3 Hermetic Library, "On the Gods and the World by Sallustius, Part 1," last modified August 26, 2017, https://hermetic.com/texts/on_the_gods-1.

streamed directly to phones and computers. We also launched department-specific social media accounts for every hotel, department, and restaurant, and offered digital marketing training to help each unit build its own small editing team. The goal wasn't just communication—it was community. We wanted frontline colleagues to share content, exchange ideas, and learn from one another.

The following year, even with less funding, we continued to invest in growth. In July and August, we launched a new series of classes—this time taught by our own colleagues. The shift to small interactive Zoom classes of five to ten students made learning more intimate, engaging, and effective. Over one thousand colleagues participated, logging more than one hundred thousand collective hours of learning.

The HR department offered over twenty courses, covering everything from hotel design and revenue management to cruise butler case studies, marketing trends, and business-report analysis. Each person was also required to take at least one cross-departmental course to broaden their horizons. The response was inspiring. Courses filled quickly. Colleagues came eager to learn, collaborate, and stretch themselves—despite the personal and professional pressures of the pandemic. Regent Taipei never stopped moving forward, and neither did the people behind it.

In the process, we uncovered something unexpected: Many of our team members knew more about international destinations than they did about their own city of Taipei. To bridge that gap, we hired laid-off tour guides to lead immersive neighborhood walks—helping our staff connect with the rich culture and hidden stories just beyond our doors. What began as a training exercise became something more: a way to see home with new eyes.

Another popular course trained our staff for the digital transformation of our hotel group. Making every staff member a social media influencer not only helped our hotels extend their public profiles but also empowered our employees with new skills. This pivot toward digitalization has continued to this day, with outside professionals brought in to teach our staff how to take good iPhone photos and other ways to appeal to a younger demographic. One member of our team became an influencer with twenty thousand followers.

Most important during this period was cross-training, which helped our employees gain competence in areas outside of their official responsibilities. At that time, we had no idea how important this training would actually be, but when we later repositioned the hotel as a destination cruise, the multiple skills our staff had gained in the cross-training courses set the foundation for the successful repositioning that kept Regent Taipei afloat.

Regent Talk, our weekly video forum, used questions to share knowledge and insights that would maintain positive momentum during this challenging time. The significant changes we undertook during that time required as much effort as opening a whole new hotel. We decided, accordingly, to recast Regent Taipei's thirtieth anniversary as year one of the hotel's rebirth and new way forward.

The Four Pillars of Leadership Development

Inspired by this culture of shared learning, my true passion lies in shared learning, creation, and well-being. It is with this same spirit of co-learning and cocreation that we officially renamed our internal platform Regent Hotel Academy in December 2021. Our focus is on fostering a culture of well-being and personal growth, guided by our principle of empathy: to serve others as we wish to be served. The Academy reflects our commitment to empowering our team members to reach their full potential through our four pillars of leadership development:

Co-learning: Developing a capacity for self-awareness; understanding your strengths, weaknesses, values, and vision; and, in a constantly changing future, being able to adapt and innovate, learn collaboratively with your team, and strive to surpass yourself every single day.

Cocreating: Continuously optimizing everything we do and creating collaboratively so that we, our families, and our guests can live more securely and happily; pursuing comprehensive well-being and aiming to present our best to Taiwan and the world.

Co-thriving: Caring for society with a positive and empathetic attitude to fulfill our corporate social responsibilities and environmental, social, and governance (ESG) commitments; pulling together SHG's core advantages to promote sustainable growth.

Empathy: Making positive energy, enthusiasm, and empathy the wellspring of all thought and the guide for action to the greatest extent possible; measuring our own success in terms of helping others to thrive.

These four principles create a lasting source of shared energy and positivity. Shaking off the zero-sum mindset—where one person's win comes at another's expense—lets us focus instead on mutual benefit and collaboration, both of which are essential for survival in a post-pandemic world.

A prime example of this philosophy is Ellen Chang, executive director of marketing and communications for SHG. After nearly thirty years with Regent Taipei, Ellen was intimately familiar with the cycles of seasonal promotions and the boilerplate expectations of a major hotel group. But within SHG, she found herself constantly innovating rather than repeating. She reinvented herself as a digital marketing expert and is now stepping into the role of our in-house AI champion.

"People who stay with SHG are the kind who want to keep learning new things and branching out, instead of just punching the time clock and waiting for instructions from headquarters," she says. "Our group retains and inspires people who appreciate a corporate culture of constantly moving to a new level." Ellen is a true Regent in every way.

These leadership principles became especially critical in the face of the pandemic, when uncertainty and fear could easily have paralyzed our organization. Instead, empowered by shared purpose and a renewed commitment to learning, our team rallied around a bold idea—one that would reimagine not just our operations but the entire guest experience.

Cocreation Culture

Discovering the key to building a learning organization was a pivotal moment for me. It wasn't about the amount of time invested but rather a matter of establishing a collaborative mechanism that could create the Medici effect.

The Medici family was known for its significant contributions to the arts in Florence during the Middle Ages by sponsoring and attracting talent from cultural fields such as painting, architecture, poetry, sculpture, and music. Additionally supported by venues and abundant funds, Florence became the birthplace of the Renaissance, which spread throughout Europe and became a glorious era in human history.

An organization that fosters shared learning becomes a vessel for creating the Medici effect. Through the interaction of different cultures, knowledge, and expertise on the same platform, we can produce amazing innovations. That's why we've integrated multifunctional and succession planning programs into our leadership training mechanism in SHG in the post-pandemic era to establish the Medici effect across brands, ranks, and hotels.

Over the past three decades, our profit center system has fostered a "unit owner" mentality in every employee—crucial for maintaining excellence in our complex industry. But the pandemic required evolving this individual accountability into collaborative teamwork geared toward cocreation and learning in a hyperspeed project system.

Our employees embraced the shift—trying new approaches, refining the old—and turned our hotels into models of recovery for the hotel industry in Taiwan and the rest of the world.

The culture of learning and collaboration at Regent Taipei was a driving force behind the company's remarkable turnaround. Numerous project teams were formed, and many innovative ideas came from the bottom up. For example, ideas for our F&B business were quickly brought to market with an emphasis on "take Regent home" and providing customers with a variety of choices, just like in our restaurants. We held weekly marketing and planning meetings to ensure that proposals rolled out continuously, without delay.

The project system broke down departmental boundaries, allowing employees to discover hidden skills and expertise in their colleagues. This cross-departmental collaboration honed project collaboration and planning skills, and it cultivated project leaders to serve as our next-generation leaders.

Empathy as a Guiding Principle

Throughout this transformation, one value consistently guided us: empathy. It informed not only how we served our guests but also how we treated one another—as learners, collaborators, and human beings. The Regent Academy wasn't just about upskilling; it was about understanding and supporting each other's growth.

Empathy had long been part of our DNA, as explored in earlier chapters, but it became essential during the uncertainty of the pandemic. Leaders and frontline staff alike had to imagine what others were experiencing, often under stress, and respond with care and creativity.

In this way, empathy became more than a principle—it became a practice embedded into how we co-learned, cocreated, and co-thrived.

The Land-Based Cruise Revolution

If there's anything I've learned from the COVID-19 crisis, it is the truth of the Chinese philosopher Laozi's saying: "Blessing coexists with adversity."[4] Once we understand that change is inherent in all things, we can understand crisis as an opportunity for change and a renewed mindset as the creator of miracles.

Our greatest initial challenge in 2020 was to realign a team that had spent thirty years catering to international business travelers so we could meet the new demand for domestic urban resorts and reposition Regent Taipei as such. Prior to the pandemic, international guests accounted for over 85 percent of Regent Taipei's bookings, so with borders shut to international travel, our greatest challenge was filling rooms. We launched countermeasures such as the thirty-six-hour Regent staycation package deal and Twin-City hotel stays, but while these promotional offers helped maintain team momentum through the first several months, their deeply discounted prices did little to offset our mounting losses.

Transformative change was the only option going forward. As I sat in regular meetings with senior executives from our group's hotels, I became increasingly aware of the dire situation faced by other five-star hotels in Taiwan. Regent Taipei was still performing

4 Laozi, *Tao Te Ching*, translated by D. C. Lau (Penguin Books, 1963).

relatively well, with occupancy rates of 60 percent on weekends and slightly below 30 percent on weekdays, but other hotels' occupancy rates were in the single digits.

Rather than rest on our laurels and risk falling into cutthroat price competition for the remaining traditional market demand, we would do better to change course early and transform Regent Taipei into the world's first "land-based cruise ship" under the "eat, drink, play, entertain, shop, and learn" framework.

This idea was initially met by quizzical stares from our hotel group executives, and their reactions weren't exactly unwarranted. There was nothing but bad news in the second quarter of 2020, and many hotels were suspending guest services and imposing massive staff layoffs, even in Taiwan, where new infections were being successfully contained. It was a challenging environment for introducing a brand-new land-based cruise experience.

The idea came to me one sleepless night that one of our Regent affiliates, Regent Seven Seas Cruise (RSSC), could help guide us through the transition. The entertainment and excitement offered on luxury cruise ships inspired me to frame our new urban resort experience in terms of the cruise vacation model. The cruise vacation experience is anything but boring, and aren't modern cruise ships even known as floating hotels?

I invited my colleagues to reimagine Regent Taipei as an enormous cruise ship. "Doesn't it actually look like one, if viewed from the front entrance at Zhongshan North Road toward the surrounding parks? Besides that, we can draw on our experience with our RSSC affiliate to create an unforgettable and all-encompassing holiday experience for our guests." When I saw heads start to nod, I began going into the specifics, knowing that clear communication was vital at a time when people could easily succumb to panic.

"Cruise ships are specifically designed to deliver memorable experiences in eating, drinking, entertaining, shopping, and learning to their clients," I pointed out. "Here at Regent Taipei, we have the Regent Galleria in the lower levels, ten high-end restaurants throughout the hotel, live performances every night, award-winning spa facilities on the twentieth floor, a rooftop pool, and gym facilities. If we add in a few more themed cultural activities around the world, along with some learning programs, we'll have all of the ingredients for a luxury cruise experience at Regent Taipei."

The learning experiences in particular would make us stand out in a way that would attract guests and boost return rates.

Making the Vision Reality

I rallied my executives to form an interdepartmental team that would devise ways to transform Regent Taipei from a hotel into a land-based luxury cruise liner that made best use of our existing facilities. Working with efficiency and dedication, my team accomplished the monumental task in under a month, launching our maiden voyage in July 2020. It's a feat that still amazes me to this day.

Launching our new cruise vacation business model in the middle of summer, we naturally focused on family-friendly activities and programs. Our goal was to create a full-service experience at Regent Taipei, complete with a family fun learning center, kids' playroom, and even colorful vending carts handing out sweets and candies. We aimed to cater to all our guests' needs with a twenty-four-hour lounge, happy-hour specials, evening movies shown under the stars next to Regent's rooftop swimming pool, herbal spa services, live performances by popular entertainers, cultural tours of the city, artists-in-residence, and dozens of engaging children's activities. Our ultimate goal was to keep kids entertained and parents free to enjoy other things.

Crisis led Regent Taipei to comprehensively restructure for future advantage and innovation. During the pandemic, the hotel was quickly transformed into the world's first land-based cruise ship, offering guests dozens of fun activities to choose from, including the starlight outdoor theater at Regent Taipei's rooftop pool. The fireworks in the background complemented our "Loveboat" cruise program.

The response to Regent Taipei's maiden cruise voyage exceeded all our expectations. In the first week alone, we filled five hundred rooms and took reservations for another five hundred. Our Sunday cruise brunch, included in the full-service cruise package, attracted well over 1,200 guests. We noticed that our cruise guests tended to arrive early and check out late, with stays distributed relatively evenly throughout the week. Likewise, we found that people lingered longer over their meals. After all, they had nowhere else to go! That made the additional cruise activities even more attractive.

To tap into this new market, we partnered with reputable travel agencies and recruited social media influencers and key opinion leaders to amplify our core marketing messages. We also tasked each department with developing and maintaining its own social media fan base.

This success belonged to the entire Regent Taipei team. We learned together by doing, discussed and reviewed results daily, and steadily improved our land cruise operations with each passing week. Innovation requires absolute candor in order to identify and resolve shortcomings as soon as possible, so rather than targeting perfection in this first phase of our new venture, our goal was simply to find ways to do things better.

One of our more memorable lessons came when we organized a treasure hunt for children in the Regent Galleria. We quickly realized that it wasn't a great idea to have dozens of kids diving into Chanel displays, and we radically scaled the event back to something more realistic. We made more mistakes than ever before, but no real damage was done, and we not only learned from the mistakes but sometimes even had fun in the process.

Innovation requires accepting error and failure. In fact, learning from missteps is more valuable than holding firmly to a preset plan. Human progress is built on the foundation of trial and error. Failures, once tried and set aside, confidently pave the way forward. In my younger years, my mistakes were points of nagging annoyance. Now, I see them as precious gifts. What actually held me back was my attitude toward them. In leading my team through the process of innovation, I never expect perfection on a first try. Perfection comes only after constant refinement and challenge.

Expanding the Cruise Experience

Facing the harsh reality of closed borders as the pandemic swept across the globe, Regent Taipei found a lifeline in its summer cruise program, which kept our 538-room hotel afloat during that trying time. The success of this innovation gave us the confidence to continue our novel approach to transformation. In the hospitality industry, guest rooms are like a hotel's production capacity, and our overreliance on international business travelers and tourists left us vulnerable. Our plummeting occupancy rates at the onset of the border quarantine restrictions made us confront the reality that we'd placed too many eggs in one basket and reminded us of the urgent need to reimagine our business.

Transforming Regent Taipei into an urban resort reminded me of my father's experience in shipbreaking, in that it required breaking out of our old comfort zones, launching into new territory, and disassembling and reassembling our business from the bottom up to meet new market expectations and needs. With the pandemic cutting us off from our most profitable customers, it was time to wield our impeccable human-centric service capabilities to cultivate new customers as stakeholders in the future of Regent Taipei.

As our new cruise-inspired concept gained momentum, we carried out a bold transformation in September: Regent Taipei became five distinct hotels in one, each tailored to a specific type of traveler. We designated the fifth and sixth floors' rooms with balconies for family guests, the seventh through tenth for domestic tour groups, and the eleventh through seventeenth for individual vacationers. The Tai Pan Residence & Club on the eighteenth and nineteenth floors offered an elite Regent Taipei experience, while the twentieth-floor Wellspring Spa expanded to include ten new Spa Villas for our most discerning guests.

To deepen the experience, I invited Regent Taipei's international team—from Japan, the United States, and Europe—to help imagine new "cruise itineraries" inspired by major cultural festivals and global traditions. What followed was a true creative exchange. The ideas came pouring in: a Tokyo-themed cruise, moon festivals around Asia, and Christmas around the world. The diverse perspectives shaped the design of our programs, turning the process itself into a shared act of discovery.

The response to our land-based cruise model exceeded all expectations. Staff and guests alike embraced the new vision with enthusiasm, proving that even in the most difficult times, innovation and teamwork can spark something entirely new—and deeply meaningful. The success of this concept showed that creativity, when paired with trust and execution, could drive not just recovery but reinvention. Yet, even as we celebrated these early wins, we knew our next move would carry even greater risk—and demand even greater courage.

A Bold Gamble Pays Off

As the pandemic continued to intensify and the Taiwan Centers for Disease Control imposed stricter response measures in mid-May 2021 and closed the hotels, our revenues went into free fall once again. With our main revenue streams severely impacted, I made the difficult but necessary decision to sell the group's lucrative Domino's Pizza franchise. We had grown the Taiwan operation from just 45 outlets to 180, gaining a full return on our original investment. Now, the NT$1.7 billion (roughly US$57 million) in cash from the sale would help ensure Regent Taipei's ability to pay our staff and protect our shareholders during the crisis.

The opportunity arrived with impeccable timing. In early 2021, Australia-based Domino's Pizza Enterprises approached me through Scott Oelkers, then vice chairman of Domino's Pizza Taiwan. Scott was the founder and had been the public face of the brand since its early days and had remained with us after we acquired the franchise in 2007. Responding to their inquiry, I calculated an asking price based on Domino's Taiwan's 2020 net profit (NT$68 million) multiplied by the current price-to-earnings ratio of Regent Taipei stock

(25). I expected negotiations—but they surprised me by quickly and enthusiastically accepting the NT$1.7 billion figure. We announced the sale on June 11.

I saw the sale as a triple win. The Taiwan franchise would move forward with stronger backing from the largest Domino's master franchisee in the world. The Australian buyer would expand its Asian footprint without diluting earnings or multiples. And for us, the infusion of cash would protect jobs, stabilize our operations, and reassure our investors during one of the most uncertain times in our company's history.

With NT$1.7 billion added to our reserves, we gained access to an additional NT$2 billion in bank lines—enough to sustain us for two to three more years through a worsening pandemic. More than just a business deal, it was a lifeline that bought us time to survive, adapt, and continue taking care of our people.

All of these measures reflected our recognition that Regent Taipei's employees were its greatest asset. Anything else could be sold off to ensure the group's survival. Material things could always be bought back, but talent and loyalty had to be nurtured and earned. The employees of Regent rewarded us with their enthusiasm and dedication in responding to the pandemic crisis and by dedicating themselves to our long-term vision for Regent Taipei.

In just three days, the executive team at Regent Taipei developed a bold plan to transform the idle restaurant and catering divisions into a new online platform called Take Regent Home. This platform offered customers a variety of gourmet menu items for fresh and hot delivery or pick-up, as well as quick-frozen and shelf-stable gourmet food gift items tailored to the at-home meal needs of families during the height of COVID-19. With our experience with Domino's and excellent execution, high-quality and affordable pricing made Regent Taipei's offerings an instant hit.

Collaborating Across the Hotel Group

Before the pandemic, domestic travelers had accounted for only around 10 to 15 percent of Regent Taipei's guest services business, so our team had much to learn and overcome in order to realign our "ship" to service the needs of the domestic travel market.

Fortunately, we had sister hotels well-experienced in the domestic travel business to support us along the way. Regent Taipei had long been a pillar of support and guidance for its sister hotels across the country. Now that we were embarking on our journey of transformation, we found ourselves needing the assistance of our fellow Silks Place hotels, including Silks Place Tainan, Silks Place Taroko, and Wellspring by Silks. Reaching out with humility, we were met with open arms and invaluable insights. Senior executives such as Cindy Chen, GM of Just Sleep and Wellspring by Silks, and Jackie Chao, GM of Silks Place Taroko, not only attended our marketing meetings but also shared their firsthand experience of successfully catering to the domestic travel market. Their teams engaged with our staff and provided real-life case studies that inspired us to keep pushing forward.

I had initially launched the Silks and Just Sleep brands with the clear mission of serving domestic travelers. It had never occurred to me that Regent Taipei would one day need to depend on our sister brands, learning from and supporting each other in ways I could never have imagined. Our teams shared experiences, crossed departments and properties, and cocreated new projects that surpassed anything we had done in the past. The pandemic that could have spelled disaster for Regent Taipei instead became a catalyst for transformation.

By veering off the path of price wars and layoffs, we found renewed purpose and direction that allowed us to not only break even but even turn a handsome profit against all odds. This newfound sense of camaraderie within our hotel group had a ripple effect that brought double-digit growth to our sister properties from the holiday-themed promotions and incentives they cocreated. Ultimately, our success was a testament to the power of collaboration and shared purpose.

The Level 3 Lockdown Challenge

Life has taught me that success is often influenced by factors outside of our control, such as timing, location, and other people. Even so, I've found that teamwork can make all the difference in tipping the odds in our favor in the face of daunting challenges.

Looking back, I find that the moments that truly fill me with pride are not the countless awards our organization has won over the years but rather the ways in which we have responded to crises. Our hotel group has dedicated itself to cocreating and transforming our way through SARS, COVID-19, and any other obstacle we've encountered.

During the COVID-19 pandemic, our hotel group saw an opportunity to cultivate a new generation of leaders capable of steering us into the future. One shining example is Edward Yew, the leasing director at Regent Galleria, who had previously served as my special assistant. In 2018, I entrusted him with repositioning Regent Galleria to appeal to younger and affluent second-generation clientele. Edward's efforts paid off tremendously during the pandemic, as he secured new leasing contracts with leading international brands and Michelin-starred restaurants and chefs, delivering annual revenues exceeding NT$8 billion by 2024.

Having survived the first blow from COVID-19 by launching our urban cruise experience in 2020, we didn't realize that the worst of the pandemic was yet to come. The blanket ban that the government issued on in-restaurant dining and food services in mid-May 2021 dealt a severe blow to our main revenue streams. As an international hotel, our staff salaries typically accounted for 30 percent of our revenues, so losing 90 percent of our revenues left us unable to cover even our salary commitments, let alone expenses for ingredients, administration, and marketing. Looking over our balance sheets, we calculated that we could continue operating for just three months before running out of cash.

This estimate of three months was based on research I had conducted on how countries with healthcare systems similar to Taiwan—such as Singapore and South Korea—had weathered their lockdowns over the previous year and a half. I had learned that lockdowns typically lasted two to three months, which gave me hope that Taiwan's restrictions might be lifted by mid-August.

While coming to terms with having to essentially shut down our hotels, I found solace in the fact that Taiwan was not alone in facing this challenge. Many other countries had already endured multiple lockdowns and had learned valuable lessons from their experiences. With so much knowledge to draw from and improve upon, I realized there was no need to succumb to despair in the face of our predicament.

During my research, I came across a fascinating statistic that provided me with valuable insights. Restaurants operating under COVID-19 lockdowns in other countries were able to resume most of their pre-lockdown monthly revenue in an average of six months. This revelation prompted me to contemplate our next moves. How would the transition be carried out? What would our focus be? What goals should we set?

Finding Hope in Crisis

With the two critical timelines of three and six months in mind, I realized that we couldn't afford any missteps. Our priority was to safeguard our employees' livelihoods and maximize cash flow. With that in mind, I decided to expedite our planned sale of the Domino's Pizza franchise in Taiwan to ensure we had enough reserves to give us a lifeline. The timing of this transaction turned out to be remarkably fortunate, providing us with critical liquidity just as the most severe lockdown measures were announced. That lifeline allowed us to safeguard jobs and keep the lights on while many of our peers were being forced to shut down.

Despite our own success in weathering the storm, I was troubled by the challenges faced by other hotels and eating establishments. Given the interdependence of the hospitality industry, the loss of international tourists could cause companies to close down and leave countless employees jobless. Our hotel group might survive for the time being, but without acting to support the industry as a whole, we might reach the end of the pandemic to find Taiwan's tourism industry shattered beyond repair. Our erstwhile competitors therefore became our allies in a shared struggle for survival.

By 2021, Taiwan's tourism industry was in an even more precarious position than the year before. Despite the government's efforts to provide assistance, we needed further action to support our severely wounded industry. As level 3 pandemic restrictions were imposed, it seemed that every sector of the economy needed the limited public aid available.

It was analogous to how COVID-19 cases were handled at that time: When case numbers were low and medical resources were plentiful, every patient with COVID-19 received dedicated care in hospital isolation wards. However, when medical resources fell short of demand, only the most serious cases were treated in isolation wards, while the remainder were monitored in quarantine hotel rooms. I appealed to the government to rescue the hotel industry with emergency subsidies. This was the only way to save as many jobs as possible, and I felt a responsibility to take a public stand.

Advocacy and Innovation

As the severity of the COVID-19 outbreak became apparent in March 2020, I felt an urge to take action in a way I had never done before. I became a public advocate for our struggling industry.

With the guidance of Henry Kao, an independent board member of SHG, I found myself sitting across from Taiwan Visitors Association Chairperson Yeh Chu-lan to discuss the dire state of the tourism industry. As we delved into the gravity of the situation, I emphasized the urgent need for government assistance, stressing that any delay could result in irreversible damage. As chair of the China Airlines' Catering company, whose revenue had also dropped by 90 percent, Yeh Chu-lan grasped the urgency immediately.

Yeh Chu-lan quickly arranged a meeting with hotel CEOs and presidents on March 8 to discuss a unified position. That same evening, she took me to meet with then Minister of Transportation and Communications, Lin Chia-lung. Armed with a detailed spreadsheet showcasing the financial support that governments in Europe and the United States were giving their struggling industries, I proposed an aggressive subsidy program aimed at providing relief in three critical areas: salaries, taxes, and property rental fees.

I underscored the importance of a comprehensive relief program by comparing the tourism industry to an ICU patient in need of immediate attention. The collapse of the tourism sector would lead to catastrophic layoffs and economic instability across other industries because of our labor intensity and large employment base. Proactive stabilization of the tourism sector was essential for Taiwan's hopes of achieving a swift post-pandemic economic recovery.

It was a humbling experience for someone who had never imagined having to make a request for government assistance, but I knew it was necessary to ensure the long-term health of our industry and the livelihoods of our staff. Despite the psychological hurdles, the resulting relief program brought a sense of security and hope to our industry during one of its darkest moments. The following year, I would return to do it all over again, knowing that the impact of the pandemic would continue to reverberate for some time to come.

Our advocacy extended beyond our group and the hospitality industry to assist the hotel's partners in weathering the financial crisis. CFO Dick Lin interceded with banks on behalf of many of our outside contractors and suppliers so they could secure loans and stay in business. More than basic empathy, we had a vested interest in helping companies with which we had built long-term relationships of trust—rather than having to start over with new vendors once the pandemic passed.

We also partnered with innovative system companies using LED light emission and other novel technology in ventilation systems to kill viruses in mutual promotion efforts that raised public awareness and helped guests feel safer returning to our hotel. These bonds, forged in adversity, strengthened all of us. In the end, our commitment to shared survival created something more lasting than recovery—it created resilience.

Digital Transformation: Take Regent Home

Seizing the Opportunity for Change

In times of crisis, I believe in doing more than just persevering. It's an opportunity to prepare for transformative change and to come out stronger on the other side. That's exactly what we did at Regent Taipei when the pandemic hit.

When the pandemic continued to intensify and the Taiwan Centers for Disease Control imposed stricter pandemic response measures in mid-May 2021, revenues went into free fall once again.

With all restaurant and room operations shut down, we faced an existential threat. In just three days, the executive team at Regent Taipei developed a bold plan to transform the idle restaurant and catering divisions into a new online platform called Take Regent Home. It offered customers a selection of freshly prepared meals as well as various frozen and shelf-stable food items.

The team was initially skeptical, but I had observed the success of this strategy in the US, where restaurants that adapted their business models from dine-in to take-out were able to restore their revenues to pre-lockdown levels in an average of six months. With our experience with Domino's and excellent execution, high-quality and affordable pricing made Regent Taipei's offerings an instant hit. Our take-out dishes were so popular that we had to coordinate with the local police department to manage the traffic around our hotel.

We had actually started working on a digital transformation of our F&B services in August 2020, anticipating that a restaurant lockdown was inevitable. When the lockdown eventually hit in May 2021, we were able to get the system online to launch a Take Regent Home website that seamlessly integrated online and offline food deliveries and pickup.

The pandemic provided the impetus for implementing a plan I'd had in mind for five years to digitally transform Regent Taipei. Within a month, we'd reconfigured our commercial kitchens, implemented health and safety protocols, and launched the Take Regent Home website.

It was a prime example of how a crisis refocuses our priorities and compels us to take action on issues that we know truly deserve our attention—but which often get pushed aside amid the distractions of maintaining the status quo.

By digitalizing our services and reaching out to a potential clientele outside the hotel's walls, we not only survived the worst of the pandemic's impact; we also opened up new horizons and possibilities for Regent Taipei to evolve with changing lifestyles and expectations in the years to come.

Building the Infrastructure

I saw the suspension of restaurant dining as an opportunity to evolve and level up our services. We were already ahead of the game with our digital transformation of rooms and accommodation in 2020, and now it was time to do the same for our restaurants. Although we were promoting takeout and delivery, we wanted to create a true online/offline service that would put Regent Taipei's restaurants back into the game.

In 2020, the stability of our restaurant business allowed us to launch our cruise project on the rooms division, but the 2021 level 3 lockdown forced us to shut down all restaurant and room operations. We now found ourselves relying on our Take Regent Home food take-out and delivery service for 90 percent of our revenue. With the entire hotel facing unprecedented challenges, we had to come together and try something new while remaining humble and focused on serving our customers in the best way possible. We were truly all in the same boat now.

We prepared for the launch of the Take Regent Home online e-commerce platform by centralizing our previously independent Chinese and Western food-service teams and profit centers. Our Brasserie buffet and the entire ground floor Azie atrium cafe became a giant logistics center where our restaurant staff gathered to sort the food from each of the hotel's eight kitchens. We also mobilized our room team members to box, deliver, and pick up food.

The website featured daily specials, weekly promotions, festivals, and a variety of delivery options, all designed to attract customers and create excitement around our brand. The platform gave us access to a new range of customers. Regent Taipei's five-star image had discouraged some people from spending money with us because they assumed we were too expensive. Our lunch boxes maintained a five-star presentation but at starting prices only slightly higher than other take-out offerings. This made many people willing to give us a try—and won us a new and broader following.

The immediate results surpassed even what I had hoped. Revenues had plummeted to 20 percent of pre-pandemic levels, but thanks to the dedication and hard effort of the entire Regent Taipei team, our revenues for June doubled to 40 percent of pre-pandemic levels. Take Regent Home grew at an incredible pace, with revenues reaching 80 percent by the end of its third month.

Creating a New Visual Identity

The digital world is inherently visual. As we embraced digitalization, I discovered that my experience working with designers on hotel projects gave me a unique perspective on visual arts—and that empathy was the key to capturing our customers' expectations and desires through design. We needed to see our branding and other visuals through the eyes of our customers and anticipate their impressions.

During our digital transformation in the COVID-19 pandemic, I encouraged the team to act like a molting caterpillar—discarding old mental habits and embracing new methods of collaborative creativity. That mindset shift was essential not only for the transformation of our online presence but also for our organization's evolution as a whole.

When level 3 pandemic controls were announced, I eagerly joined Regent Taipei's online platform development team as their visual director. Together, we set out to cocreate the hotel's digital presence and design a website that would reflect our group's unique identity. Through the process, I learned that while aesthetics mattered, it wasn't the highest priority. Our first version of the website was overly elegant—but we quickly realized it had to communicate clearly and intuitively to meet real user needs in a digital space.

We knew that we wanted to retain our simple yet elegant brand image, but we needed to translate that elegance into more streamlined and direct consumer messaging. It was like removing the varnish and exposing our singularly graceful grain. This process allowed us to reinterpret the hotel's richly textured elegance from the physical world into a digital form, which was an exciting and rewarding challenge.

Data-Driven Innovation Through Co-Learning

A bonus of the Take Regent Home platform was that it built up a database on customer demand and preferences. We used data analysis to continually improve the program and keep it fresh, and this data has continued to help us develop products and anticipate demand in the years since the pandemic.

This digital transformation had a profound impact on Regent Taipei, both internally and externally. It allowed our employees to tap into their full potential and become creators and salespeople. By challenging ourselves and working together, we were able to generate as much revenue in four months as the top five hotels in the city combined.

Connecting the online platform to the offline service value chain required the full commitment and dedication of everyone on our team, regardless of their role. Our journey was akin to that of a lean start-up, with front- and back-end colleagues rolling up their sleeves and supporting each other to complete impossible tasks. Although the process was challenging, it was also filled with the joy of collaborative learning.

For example, creating the perfect dish is an art form that takes time, energy, and craftsmanship, as we know all too well at Take Regent Home. When we set out to recreate the signature Empress Lobster Stock with King Crab Meat and Seafood from Silks House, we knew we were in for a challenge. This dish, with its orange-red hue and delicately fragrant steam, is a true masterpiece that requires three hours of preparing the lobster stock and cooking the key ingredients in the precise order.

At first, the chefs were concerned that the taste of the dish would be compromised due to long delivery times. This is where our in-house delivery team became critical. Drawing from our experience in operating Domino's Pizza, Silks House quickly established a delivery team to ensure that the dish was delivered freshly and promptly.

We realized that if customers were raving about our signature dish, some might want to recreate it at home. Guided by empathy and our commitment to treating others as we'd wish to be treated, we created a ready-to-cook package: completed broth, fresh king crab meat and seafood ingredients, pre-fried Thai fragrant rice, and an online tutorial featuring Chef Wu. With a quick boil and a few simple steps, the dish could be ready in ten minutes. Customers told us the quality almost matched the in-restaurant experience—which gave us the confidence to expand our take-out and delivery offerings to other gourmet dishes previously thought to be impossible to serve outside of restaurants, such as Peking duck and tomahawk steak.

This same spirit of collaboration sparked a bold idea for reimagining the hotel's vacant presidential suite. Our guest room and F&B teams joined forces to create the Michelin Star Journey—a luxury overnight experience with twenty-four-hour butler service in the Taipan Lounge and private dinners prepared by Michelin-starred chefs inside the suite itself. It transformed an underused space into something intimate, exclusive, and unforgettable.

Regent Taipei's TaiPan Residence & Club was Taiwan's first all-butler hotel, providing a host of exclusive, personalized guest services and a twenty-four-hour butler on call.

Looking back, the digital transformation didn't just help us survive a crisis—it gave us a long-term growth engine. Regent Taipei's creative response helped set the pace for the industry and offered a path forward for others. Restaurants across Taiwan soon adopted online ordering systems modeled after ours. In the process, we became an unlikely role model for resilience—and a beacon of recovery and renewal.

Looking Back with Gratitude

While the resilience of Regent Taipei's team was apparent during the first year of the pandemic, it truly shone during the 2021 lockdown as we embarked on our incredible journey of cocreation and innovation, launching numerous new programs and projects. Our senior executives led by example, tirelessly co-learning and cocreating with their staff, which ultimately resulted in what I call the Regent Taipei miracle. Not only did we speak out for our industry and society; we also strengthened our connection to Taiwan's culture and heritage. Additionally, we established an industry-wide platform that demonstrated our commitment to collaboration and community-building.

At the heart of it all was the empathy that had become a core value of our organization and which we effectively employed at the individual, departmental, and organizational levels. This approach allowed us to launch a resolute and progressively triumphant counter-offensive, ensuring that our hotel group emerged from the pandemic stronger than ever. Empathy now shaped not only how we perceived and related to our customers but also how we worked with one another within our team.

Thanksgiving 2021 held special significance for me as I reflected on all that I had to be thankful for. Throughout the challenges of the pandemic, the unwavering support of Taiwan's society had been a source of great comfort and strength. It wasn't just the community that had rallied behind our hotels—it was also the colleagues, customers, partners, shareholders, friends, and family members whose full trust and support enabled us to transform a year of dire crisis into one of positive transformation.

As I reflect on Regent Taipei's journey through the pandemic crisis, it becomes clear that our transformation and creative response not only set the pace for our industry but also inspired businesses across various sectors. For example, the restaurant sector quickly picked up on our adoption of online take-out orders. It's humbling to see how our example has been studied and utilized to embark on transformative journeys across different industries. Perhaps our success shows that a pandemic does not have to be an economic death sentence.

The challenges of the pandemic tested every aspect of our organization, from our financial resilience to our creative capacity, from our leadership team to our frontline employees. What emerged was not just a survivor but a transformed organization that had discovered new ways to serve our community and new technologies.

Rather than merely persevering, I have learned to embrace crisis as an invaluable opportunity to shake off self-imposed encumbrances and limitations and reimagine the best path forward.

The Sweetness of Hard-Won Victories

"Welcome aboard Regent Taipei Cruise, and enjoy our simulated Tokyo vacation experience!"

As I entered our suite, I felt enveloped by an ambiance of Japanese culture as our Japanese butler helped us change into traditional *yukata* robes and immerse ourselves in a serene tea ceremony. As my wife, Constance, and I donned our Japanese yukata for a leisurely stroll through the Regent Galleria, I expected to feel a bit awkward, but to my surprise, I felt as if we were actually on vacation. We then proceeded to a delectable Wagyu shabu-shabu dinner and sipped sake at the Dasai bar in our very own Mihan Japanese restaurant at B3. It was easy to forget that we weren't in Tokyo but rather at the Regent Taipei.

The next day, we took part in a themed experience at the Brasserie buffet restaurant, which recreated Japan's famed Tsukiji Fish Market with daily fresh seafood from Taiwan's east coast. Our Japanese team added authenticity and depth to the dining experience by enthusiastically sharing descriptions of the day's catch along with the rules and hand signals used in bidding in the fish auction to avoid the distraction of loud noises in the marketplace.

These unforgettable activities were part of Regent Taipei's innovative cruise vacation package, held during the hotel's inaugural land cruise season in the midst of the COVID-19 pandemic. I'm proud to say that we were probably the first five-star hotel anywhere in the world to offer such a unique and engaging experience.

With tourism being one of the first industries to succumb to the pandemic tsunami, Regent Taipei faced unprecedented challenges from 2020 to 2021, but it was these difficult times that helped me appreciate more than ever the value of creativity in adversity.

It became clear that merely readjusting our marketing strategy would not suffice in the face of the COVID-19 pandemic. Instead, a complete overhaul of our approach to business was required to cope with plunging domestic and international tourism. That is what led me to return to the Regent's roots as an urban resort destination.

Regent's flagship Hong Kong property had set a new global standard for urban resort hotels when it first opened in 1981. With its impeccable service and floor-to-ceiling windows boasting stunning views of Victoria Harbor, the hotel was an icon of luxury.

To create an unforgettable impression, the hotel was set back several hundred meters from the main road in the busiest district of Kowloon and accessed by a winding path to the forecourt that created a serene sense of arrival seldom experienced in the bustling metropolis.*When the newly renovated Regent Hong Kong reopened in 2023, it regained its place as the Regent brand's crown jewel and fulfilled my dream of restoring this iconic Hong Kong hotel with Gaw Capital and IHG.*

This urban resort ethos is also reflected in the design of Regent Taipei, where spatial layering was used to create the hotel's widely acclaimed resort-like sense of arrival. Like Regent Hong Kong, Regent Taipei is set back from the main thoroughfare, and a gracefully curved road passes through a hundred-meter-deep forecourt adorned with manicured greenery on the way to the front entrance. The sound of a water fountain just outside the doors creates an intuitive barrier between the bustling city outside and the relaxing environment within.

The conceptual deep space design of Regent Taipei's forecourt draws on the aesthetic principle of *oku*, a concept used for centuries in Japanese Zen gardens and Shinto shrines to layer space in a way that pulls visitors inward—toward both cerebral and spiritual calm. Chinese characters have also been thoughtfully integrated into the hotel's environment—not only for their meaning but also for their visual grace. The calligraphic rendering of our Silks House Cantonese restaurant is a prime example.

In that same spirit, Regent Taipei responded to the pandemic's unprecedented impact on global tourism by proactively rethinking its core operations. With international tourism expected to be severely limited for several years, we made the decision to shift our focus to the domestic market—while keeping the door open to the eventual return of international guests. To do so, we chose to recalibrate Regent Taipei from a five-star international business hotel back to its original intention: a full-service urban resort.

History suggests that travel always finds its way back. Tourism rebounded strongly after both World Wars because people are inherently drawn to venturing out—and to bringing their experiences home. Today, the rise of virtual reality has only heightened our hunger for real-world immersion. At the same time, the pandemic has made those experiences more complex and more precious.

This has led to a growing desire for deep travel—fewer destinations, longer stays, and richer experiences. In a post-pandemic world, where logistics are harder and time feels more valuable, people are looking to get more out of every journey. That's exactly what an urban resort such as Regent Taipei is designed to offer.

I also observed that Silks Place Taroko, situated in the picturesque Taroko National Park on Taiwan's east coast, was one of the first hotels in our group to recover from the pandemic. With international travel restricted, our Taiwanese guests stayed longer, and weekday occupancy rates often exceeded our targeted maximum of 85 percent.

The pandemic allowed us to reflect on the strengths of our hotel group as well as on the future of the travel and tourism industry. This resulted in the strategic decision to fully embrace our urban resort DNA and position city hotels in the group as premier destinations for such an experience. So far, this new path has worked well for us.

It was through this ongoing self-renewal that we were able to reimagine—and implement—new strategies such as the land-based cruise concept, which had already begun reshaping our future.

Insight: Renewal as the Secret of Success

Mahler, the visionary composer who dedicated his life to exploring the meaning of existence through his music, offers us a powerful symbol of transformation in his Symphony No. 2, *Resurrection*. As biographer Gerard Specht observed, this symphony speaks to the universal fears, hopes, and doubts that shape the human experience. In our personal lives and in the world of business, we face crises that demand courage, insight, and a sense of purpose. True leaders can rise to these challenges by making wise decisions that inspire action.

Change is an inevitable force that shapes everything in the world. Birth and death, uncertainty and mystery mark our journey through life. The story of Regent Taipei–SHG embodies the power of transformation in the face of uncertainty. Through resilience and commitment to renewal, we have turned crises into opportunities for growth and evolution. This cycle of transformation forms a universal pattern of rebirth and rejuvenation that is the secret of Regent Taipei's enduring success.

Imagine our renewal system as a vast and intricate solar system. Each planet in the solar system has its own unique orbit, yet all revolve around the sun. Similarly, our renewal system has various components that contribute to its overall success.

At the heart of our system is empathy, much like the sun at the center of the solar system. The sun of empathy has fueled the renewal journey of Regent Taipei to create a lifestyle that resonates with the latest trends. This is achieved through the establishment of a learning organization, where knowledge is cultivated and shared to form the foundation of the renewal vision. With a practical hybrid business model in place, the focus has shifted to the vital element of execution power to turn the vision of renewal into a tangible action plan.

The pursuit of sustainable culture and human well-being remains the group's top priority as we strive to fulfill our mission of bringing the best of the world to Taiwan and the best of Taiwan to the world. This continuous effort cultivates a capacity for crossover innovation that allows for endless possibilities in creating a better world.

Transformation is a crucial element in how the world operates. The critical role of continuous transformation is reflected in the yin-yang tai chi symbol, which symbolizes the interconnectedness of fortune and misfortune and suggests that great fortune can sometimes bring unexpected destruction, while apparent disasters can lead to new success.

This idea is also reflected in the fifth movement of Mahler's *Resurrection*, where the mezzo-soprano's singing conveys the same truth:

O believe, my heart, oh believe,
Nothing will be lost to you
Everything is yours that you have desired,
Yours, what you have loved, what you have struggled for.
O believe,
You were not born in vain,
Have not lived in vain, suffered in vain!
What was created must perish,
What has perished must rise again.
Tremble no more,
Prepare yourself to live!

When confronting a life-threatening crisis, our contemplation extends beyond the surface-level concerns of life and death to plumb the meaning of existence itself. What does it truly mean to experience resurrection?

To navigate these weighty questions, it may be helpful to create a personal system of renewal or to engage in practices that promote personal growth and transformation, which can help us navigate these weighty questions. By bravely initiating this journey of self-discovery, we can cultivate the courage and resilience we need to face life's challenges with grace and authenticity.

Favorite Dishes

At the release event for the Taiwan-focused gourmet award "500 Dishes" in 2024, Silks House left the audience in awe by winning awards for seventeen dishes, the most won by any restaurant in the history of the awards. When the host asked me which Regent Taipei dish I would vote for if I could only choose one, I took a moment to ponder. Finally, I replied, "Robin's Salad Bar," which allows everyone to create their own personal plate with infinite variations, using the freshest produce from all over Taiwan in their purest form with artisanal salts and oils. This is the healthiest and most delicious food anyone can create for themselves.

Silks House is a restaurant that carries on the best of traditional food culture while also striving to innovate and create new culinary experiences. As someone who often receives requests for Silks House recommendations, I have compiled my first-ever list for this book. However, I urge you not to limit yourself to my suggestions but rather to use them as a starting point to explore and discover the various delicacies that Silks House has to offer. Remember, simplicity or extravagance depends on the person, so be adventurous and create your own memories.

On rare occasions, I order Silks House's Soup Pairing Water Banquet, a meal inspired by my trip to Henan several years ago with the YPO. We had the privilege of tasting the famous Luoyang Water Banquet at a century-old restaurant. Many of the dishes came as small bowls of soupy treasures with a sweet-and-sour flavor similar to traditional Taiwanese treats. When I asked the owner if the restaurant was run by Taiwanese businessmen, she nearly kicked me out. She explained that the Luoyang Water Banquet dates back to the Tang dynasty, when Empress Wu Zetian celebrated her enthronement with a banquet that included the finest dishes from the Henan and Luo River regions in Central China. Most Taiwanese people can trace their ancestors to the same region and hence share similar culinary roots one thousand miles south.

I returned with the inspiration to celebrate Taiwan's culinary soup culture in a way that would feel familiar to international guests—something like wine pairing. Offered in small teacups with each course, our soup pairings allow guests to enjoy a variety of broths that complement each dish.

In recent years, our restaurant group has actively focused on rediscovering our culinary heritage by using the freshest ingredients and traditional flavors. Chef Max Wu, renowned for his Cantonese cuisine and seafood expertise, has played a vital role in Silks House's signature dishes. They include the Empress Lobster Stock with King Crab Meat and Seafood, signature barbecued pork with honey sauce, deep-fried radish pastry, king crab three ways, crab on minced pork pie, gigantic shaved ice platters, and, my personal favorite, the braised mangrove crab roe with mapo tofu.

Fans of authentic Shanghainese cuisine will love the sautéed eel with chives and bean sprouts at Lan Ting, the Sichuan–Shanghai restaurant on the twenty-first floor of the Regent Taipei. Other must-try dishes at Lan Ting include firm tofu skin with pickled Chinese mustard greens, braised Dongpo pork, braised oxtail, braised yellow fish with garlic, as well as the mapo tofu by Japan's "Iron Chef" Chen Jianyi.

At Robin's Grill, Chef James Chen carefully selects prime bone-in beef, nearly on par with Wagyu, for the steakhouse and teppanyaki. The unbeatable taste of these mouthwatering steaks is matched with a salad bar that I can't live without. If you're looking for a dish to share with family or friends, the tomahawk steak trio is my choice. However, for non-beef eaters, I highly recommend the Spanish Ibérico Bellota pork, which I personally believe is even better tasting than some steaks. Our teppanyaki serves the freshest seafood and legendary cuts of US prime meats that are cooked to perfection.

Our sparkling Oolong Champagne Tea has replaced wine as my preferred beverage when dining. Cold brewed with Perrier to ensure that its bubbles are delicate and lasting, it is combined with the finest oolong tea leaves, Oriental Beauty, to pair perfectly with any meal or cocktail reception.

For an all-ages dining experience, head to the Brasserie buffet restaurant for its grand breakfast recommended by CNN as essential eating in Taipei. My favorite is the fresh seafood counter featuring fresh catches from Taiwan's east coast's Chenggong Fishery Harbor and the green counter by our partner Little Tree Cafe.

Those looking for something simple yet delicious should head over to Azie. This restaurant, situated in the atrium, features mouth-watering modern fusion cuisine such as pizza, pasta Bolognese, and Korean bibimbap. Our simple shrimp and scallop stir-fried rice with XO sauce is a favorite of connoisseurs.

The New York–style spicy shrimp and pork wontons in peanut butter and sesame oil are also a must-try. Always on the lookout for exceptional dishes, I couldn't resist bringing the taste of New York to the Regent when I returned from my travels. I asked our chef to develop a version that incorporates peanut sauce to lend sweetness and texture to the original thin chili sauce.

And of course, no visit to Regent Taipei is complete without sampling our award-winning Champion Beef Noodle Soup. The Braised Beef Noodles and Champion Clear Broth Beef Noodles, with their double dose of meat, are both outstanding and absolute must-haves. I make a point of keeping our frozen Double Beef Noodles in stock at home to satisfy my beef noodle cravings.

For a change of scenery, head up to the second floor and visit the Gallery Lounge. The Regent Cooler and lobster rolls are fantastic options that I always enjoy.

Those who appreciate the delicate flavors of shabu-shabu hot pot and sukiyaki have to visit Mihan Honke on the B3 level. The flavorful steamed beef, which tastes fresh from a steam room, is a particular favorite of mine. And don't miss out on the King Crab Set!

For those with a sweet tooth, Regent Taipei has you covered. The Banana Chocolate Mousse and Fruit Mille Crepe are both divine, with the labor-intensive yet refreshing taste of the crepe being particularly noteworthy. If you're looking for something whimsical, my daughter Kristen has always loved the cake pops and Hokkaido souffle milk rolls.

I also highly recommend the restaurants located in the Regent Galleria, which offer an array of culinary options, each more delectable than the last. Prime examples are Michelin-starred chef Richie Lin's Coast and Impromptu by Paul Lee. Both of these restaurants collaborated with Take Regent Home to offer exclusive online meals, such as Paul Lee's Michelin set menu featuring grilled corn-fed chicken and Richie Lin's Nanyang-style grilled ribs set. These were my family's go-to meals during the limited time they were available.

Richie also operates a Michelin-starred Japanese yakitori restaurant, Fumee, where chicken is grilled to perfection. Circum is another Michelin-starred restaurant that serves the finest modern Taiwanese cuisine with French flair, and a favorite for sophisticated international travelers.

Golden/Afterglo is the most recent addition to our collection of best-in-class restaurants in the Regent Galleria, featuring stylish Asian-inspired favorites with a luxury twist—such as fried chicken with caviar.

Regent also offers two of the greatest Parisian sweets purveyors: a Pierre Hermé boutique cafe and a Jean-Paul Hévin chocolatier. And for comfort, Tsubaki Salon from Hokkaido has a take-out souffle pancake fruit sandwich that is perfect for snacking.

Regent Taipei uses locally sourced Taiwanese ingredients to craft a range of iconic dishes.

Renowned as the "number one buffet in Taipei" for its exceptional offerings, popularity, and outstanding market reputation, Brasserie is celebrated for its daily supply of abundant and fresh seafood sourced directly from the nearby fishing harbor.

Silks Palace's "Imperial Treasures Feast" showcases exquisite dishes inspired by cultural artifacts, such as the Jadeite Cabbage, Meat-Shaped Stone, and Bitter Melon White Jade. Particularly eye-catching are the whimsical Mini Empress Dowager Longevity Buns.

The Silks House signature Empress Lobster Stock with King Crab Meat and Seafood, and its iconic, gigantic shaved-ice platter.

Many of our customers now prefer Regent Taipei's specially curated sparkling teas over traditional champagne or wine.

Silks House's signature braised mangrove crab roe with mapo tofu is a standout dish that has become a favorite among diners. This dish has garnered widespread acclaim, earning multiple domestic food awards for its delicious twist on the classic mapo tofu.

The DNA of Regent Taipei's F&B: Jean-Pierre Dosse

The pandemic brought about unprecedented challenges to the business landscape, and the closure of Taiwan's borders was no exception. However, it was during this time that the F&B department at Regent Taipei truly proved its substance through our innovative Take Regent Home platform.

As I reflect on this period, I am filled with gratitude for the foundation laid by Regent Taipei's second GM, Jean-Pierre Dosse.

Before his time at Regent Taipei, Jean-Pierre had served as global VP for F&B for the Regent brand, where he made a significant impact on the fine dining experiences of Regent properties worldwide. He opened hotel restaurants in Beverly Wilshire, Sydney, Melbourne, and Auckland—and created the famous Regent Cooler, a refreshing beverage made with fresh Sunkist oranges that became a staple of the hotel's Gallery Lounge.

This drink was first served to Elizabeth Taylor and Michael Jackson during their visit to Taiwan in 1993. Jean-Pierre knew that Ms. Taylor had developed a fondness for it during her stays at the Regent Beverly Wilshire. Today, the Regent Cooler has become a signature of Regent Taipei, a reflection of our team's enduring creativity.

In addition to the innovative ideas he introduced in the 1990s, Jean-Pierre was also instrumental in resolving long-standing issues and internal conflicts. One of his most important contributions was launching the Brasserie, now considered Taiwan's premier buffet venue.

My former boss, Chairman Chen of Tuntex, had observed strong demand for a high-quality buffet. But Jean-Pierre's predecessor resisted the idea, and the Brasserie—at the time serving à la carte Western cuisine—struggled to attract a following or generate sufficient revenue.

When Jean-Pierre arrived, he recognized the importance of adapting to the local market. He listened to feedback from ownership and the community and turned the Brasserie into a successful buffet that quickly rose to prominence.

At a time when most five-star hotels offered only three or four in-house restaurants, Jean-Pierre and his team were operating eight to ten, catering to a wide range of local dining preferences. He also embraced our profit center concept, positioning Regent Taipei's restaurants as some of the best in both the hotel and independent dining scenes.

PART II

The Inspired Entrepreneur

CHAPTER 5

Designing for Meaning

"The real voyage of discovery consists not in seeking new landscapes but in having new eyes."

—MARCEL PROUST[5]

More than just a building, a hotel is like a hidden city bustling with tales shared by an eclectic mix of people, lending character to the urban landscape.

Taiwan's unique allure stems from its vibrant people and the breathtaking landscape that nature has bestowed on it. More than 60 percent of the country is cloaked in mountains that range from tropical to subtropical zones, from sea level to towering heights of over three thousand meters. The fascinating combination of people and natural abundance invigorates distinct urban and rural styles and offers limitless possibilities for immersive travel experiences.

SHG strives for a perfect balance between humanity and nature. Particularly during the COVID-19 pandemic, the accolades the group received for its resilience and adaptability are a testament to its core values of embracing Taiwan's captivating people and abundant nature.

---

5 Proust, Marcel. *The Captive & The Fugitive*. Translated by C. K. Scott Moncrieff and Terence Kilmartin. Modern Library Classics.

The hotels of SHG each express a unique identity, shaped by their surroundings. Regent Taipei and Regent Chongqing, both located in the hearts of their respective cities, highlight the brand's planning, design, and management expertise. Silks Place Tainan reflects the artistic and historical richness of Taiwan's ancient capital, while Silks Place Taroko immerses guests in the natural grandeur of Taroko Gorge. Our Wellspring properties in Jiaoxi and Beitou celebrate Taiwan's storied hot spring culture, offering spaces of serenity and renewal.

Across our portfolio, our hotels can take on different forms. They may be international five-star icons such as Regent, urban resorts such as Silks Place, or imaginative design hotels under the Just Sleep brand that celebrate local community aesthetics. In some cases, they transform entirely—into what we call *X*, a future-facing vision that defies categorization.

Just Sleep Taipei Sanchong exemplifies this creative approach, transforming a former lumber mill into an industrial-chic hotel full of personality and local character. The concept draws from the family history of the site owner, Long Fa Lumber Mill, founded by the local mayoral family. We fused this heritage with New York SoHo sensibility to connect the local legacy to a global lifestyle: playful, raw, and tactile. The high-ceilinged lobby features a wooden ladder centerpiece, while a chandelier made from iron chains doubles as both sculpture and lighting. Even the mugs in the guest rooms come with whimsical handles shaped like screwdrivers and drills. Guests responded immediately—the hotel reached breakeven within its first month of opening.

When you step into a Silks hotel in any location, you're not just indulging in but are also entering the realm of local cultural renaissance. This is where our hotels lead the way—by breaking free from the traditional hospitality-industry framework to showcase ingenuity in value innovation.

The Just Sleep Taipei Sanchong merges SoHo industrial chic with local woodwork craftsmanship.

For us, innovation means creating new service experiences, maximizing brand added values, and providing a total solution to customers and hotel owners alike by infusing the "total lifestyle cycle" into our products and services.

Regent's comprehensive development of branded residences overseas helped establish it as a benchmark for luxury mixed-use complexes—creating a rare win–win–win for developers, customers, and the brand. The success of Regents Montenegro, Phu Quoc, Jakarta, and Boston Seaport stands as a testament to this model.

In fact, Regent Taipei pioneered the mixed-use lifestyle concept early on by combining its hotel with Regent Galleria, offering a seamless integration of luxury retail and hospitality. We later expanded our property services to include best-in-class luxury serviced residences, such as Jasper Villa Xinyi in Taipei and Shanghai's Tomson Riviera.

Staying ahead of market trends has always been a priority for SHG. One proud moment came when our approach caught the attention of my Columbia MBA alum David Chang, founder of Storm Media. David had long been a regular guest at Regent Taipei during his business trips for Goldman Sachs. After retiring as a partner, he returned to Taiwan to pursue a new vision: establishing an independent, professionally run news outlet in Taiwan's emerging media landscape.

With his deep background in finance and real estate, David recognized an opportunity to launch Taiwan's first independent real estate investment trust (REIT). He admired SHG's innovative mindset and invited us to cofound and manage the asset management firm behind the REIT. That partnership continues to this day—and David remains one of the longest-serving members of our board of directors.

Empathy has made Silks Place Yilan not just a hotel but a haven for families. Having observed his own child's love of toy cars, the owner sought to create a safe space where children could drive their own cars, leading to the creation of Taiwan's most successful "family car hotel," where kids can drive around entire hotel floors and park their chosen electric cars in the rooms. Regent Taipei also helped the hotel to launch "Red Lantern" restaurant, which has become the most popular roasted-ducks eatery in Taiwan.

The lobby of Regent Chongqing boasts a stunning design with ceramic tiles from the famous porcelain center of Jingdezhen, depicting a bird's-eye view of the staggered rooftops of Chongqing's mountain city. Additionally, the walls are adorned with decorative art showcasing local food culture, with a focus on Chongqing's renowned spicy chili peppers. Lastly, a beautiful copper wire screen designed by Taiwanese professionals and crafted by local artisans pays tribute to the city's industrial roots.

Regent Chongqing seamlessly blends local culture and craftsmanship to create a unique interpretation of Chongqing's rich history and contemporary present.

Cocreation with Local Culture

At SHG, we believe that cocreating with local culture is not just an aspect of hospitality but also a mission to connect travelers with the local community in a way that brings new meaning to collaborative and mutually beneficial travel experiences.

Recognizing the tourism industry's capacity to enrich local economies and provide job opportunities for small and medium-sized enterprises and self-employed individuals, we regard working with the local community as fundamental to the success of our hotels.

One example is our group's extensive procurement of seafood and meat. Since 2004, Regent Taipei has collaborated with Taitung's Fishing Port to deliver freshly caught seafood directly to our central kitchen. We purchase the entire catch of each boat and supply it to our various restaurants. This not only ensures steady income for local fishermen but also allows us to offer guests the freshest and most distinctive sea-to-table experiences.

Our commitment to cocreating with local culture is also essential to achieving our goal of connecting the world to the local community. To achieve this, the people of SHG use their intuition and insight to deeply explore local culture, integrate its unique elements, and design experiences that are authentic yet distinctive.

We understand that a sense of emotional familiarity and cultural connection cannot be created out of thin air. Instead, we redefine *bespoke yet familiar* as the act of injecting new life into timeless classics.

This is reflected best of all in our food offerings. One of my favorite examples is Regent Taipei's champagne tea. This nonalcoholic sparkling beverage has gained a strong following among foodie guests, many of whom have told me they prefer it to champagne. It is also a global yet local application to expand the appeal of tea to Western cocktail and gourmet circles. Likewise, we've developed a range of flavorful tea beverages and an oolong tea beer in partnership with a leading Taiwanese brewery, and it has gained a strong following in the Japanese and Hong Kong high-end restaurants and bars.

Even our Champion Beef Noodles are not immune to tweaks and improvements. While keeping our classic standard priced competitively to outside venues, we also offer upgraded versions using grilled rib eye and Wagyu beef for steak noodles.

Considering topics that are global yet local is like shooting a TV series that the whole world can enjoy. Although the program is created for a global market, it has to delve into the local culture to find a common language, and it needs to preserve local characteristics without alienating people from other countries.

Wellspring by Silks Jiaoxi is a prime example. We recognized an opportunity to create a hot-spring hotel that was more exclusive and situated adjacent to the affordable Just Sleep Jiaoxi. But how could we offer a unique experience that stood out from the twenty other hot-spring resorts in town? We decided to redefine the hot-spring culture and created a new Japanese-Taiwanese fusion hot-spring hotel, complete with luxurious hot-spring pools in each room. We wanted to cater to those who value personal privacy and allow guests to enjoy a relaxing hot-spring ritual in the tranquil atmosphere of their own rooms.

In addition, Wellspring by Silks Jiaoxi has embraced art as a way to showcase the beauty of Yilan. The hotel is a cultural platform that features works by resident artists, and the guest rooms are adorned with handmade pottery by Taiwanese ceramic artists. Our staff uniforms are made with indigo dye, a local specialty in Yilan, and we've even launched a poetry anthology inspired by the eight scenic spots of Lanyang. We invite resident artists to create works of art in Yilan throughout the year, and guests can interact with them during scheduled times in the hotel's lobby. We also offer tours to explore the hidden paths of Lanyang, taking guests on an adventure to experience the beauty of the Lanyang Plain.

SHG's passion for collaborating with local culture can be traced back to Silks Place Taroko. Here, the hotel incorporated a variety of local elements into its aesthetic and hospitality services, such as mountain hikes, whale watching, an outdoor cinema, locally sourced ingredients in its restaurants, and showcases for local art and culture.

As will be described a little later, this transformation was complicated by the fact that the property had been underperforming, operating at a loss for over a decade. In 2009, we repositioned the property with the twelve concepts of Regent Essence, and the newly renovated hotel opened under its new name—Silks Place Taroko—in 2010. It has become a profitable and cherished destination for travelers.

Before the COVID-19 pandemic, foreign guests accounted for 30 to 40 percent of the visitors to Silks Place Taroko, with many loyal clients staying for a week or longer. The hotel became a destination for admiring the stunning Taroko Gorge scenery while also finding respite and rejuvenation for mind and body. Taimei, a stray dog adopted by the hotel, quickly gained a following on social media and became a beloved resident dog among the guests. SHG recognizes that hotels of the future will no longer merely be part of the tourism economy but will also be part of the ecosystem.

Our group currently operates fifteen hotels with nearly 2,500 rooms throughout Taiwan, and we plan to grow to twenty hotels with 3,000 rooms by 2026. This includes new properties, such as the upcoming Silks X in Linkou-Taipei, along with additional Wellspring and Just Sleep hotels. We also opened our first overseas Just Sleep in Osaka's Shinsaibashi district in 2023.

Across this expanding footprint, all of our brands remain grounded in the same design and operational DNA—twelve core concepts that guide everything from layout to guest interaction. As we continue to connect global and local communities and build cultural bridges between East and West, we hold fast to the same principle: Innovation must serve meaning.

Local Wisdom, Global Welcome

The effort to bridge East and West shapes how we design spaces, orchestrate movement, and frame each guest's experience. Rather than aiming solely for comfort, we focus on creating emotional resonance—transitions that feel meaningful as well as beautiful.

Take the Regent Taipei's entrance. Unlike most urban hotels that hug the street, we set our facility back, creating a hidden oasis where guests arrive via a sweeping driveway into a calm forecourt. This spatial buffer allows the bustle of the city to fall away before one even steps inside. It's a subtle gesture but one with profound psychological effect—a chance to breathe, to pause.

Inside, this intention continues. The Silks House restaurant welcomes visitors with a white screen wall and a lone desk lamp—a Zen-inspired moment of vacancy. Further in, glass-carved calligraphy panels play with light and shadow, transforming hallways into contemplative passages. These details echo the Japanese concept of *omotenashi*: hospitality rooted in attentiveness, discretion, and restraint.

Even the timing of gestures is intentional. When a taxi arrives, our doormen wait a few seconds before opening the door—respecting the guest's need to pay, gather their belongings, and transition with dignity. It's a small difference, but it turns routine into ritual.

To us, service is about systems—but hospitality is about *presence*. Bridging East and West means bringing the world's best design principles into harmony, then layering them with a local sense of timing, texture, and emotional insight. That's what transforms a hotel from a building into a living philosophy.

This philosophy of design and timing finds its deepest resonance when it's rooted in the land and culture from which it arises.

Our connection to our land is fundamental, whether we are in Taiwan or abroad. Rooting ourselves in the land while also connecting with the world empowers us to bring the best of the world to Taiwan and the best of Taiwan to the world.

Silks House, designed by Japanese architect Yukihiro Hashimoto, offers a captivating entrance through a corridor adorned with laser-carved calligraphy in glass and enhanced by mirrors and scenic lighting, creating an immersive cultural ambience.

Over time, I realized that the planning and positioning of a hotel involves more than the design and construction of a building. Beyond the practicalities of financial planning, it requires a humanistic approach that considers the hotel's relationship with people, nature, and the environment. The concept focuses not only on internal matters but also on external factors, such as the local economy and historical and cultural issues.

I was reminded of this when I read the *Tao Te Ching* by Laozi and was struck by a quote: "The reason why heaven and earth are able to endure and continue this long is because they do not live off, or for, themselves."[6] In other words, nature is sustained by opening itself up to all living things with its boundless generosity.

6 Laozi, *Tao Te Ching*, translated by D. C. Lau (Penguin Books, 1963).

Although I recognized the appeal of this concept early on, I have only in recent years come to understand how it should be applied to business and life: In order to be truly successful, we must embrace nature and learn from nature. This mindset recognizes that we are part of nature and that coexisting is essential for enduring success.

The rebirth of Silks Place Taroko exemplifies this mindset. Under its earlier identity as Grand Formosa Tianxiang, it struggled for more than ten years with an occupancy rate of less than 50 percent. It was by shifting the focus back to working with nature that the hotel found renewed success as Silks Place Taroko.

Silks Place Taroko has deep roots in both national history and my own family's story. Originally built as the Tianxiang Lodge, a private retreat for Chiang Kai-shek, also known as "the Generalissimo," it hosted dignitaries and international guests for decades.

The hotel was operated by China Travel Service, a subsidiary of the Shanghai Commercial & Savings Bank (SCSB)—an institution closely linked to our family for three generations. My father was one of SCSB's first clients when it was reinstated in Taiwan in 1965, and he eventually became a shareholder and long-term partner. So when the newly formed Taroko National Park Headquarters invited the bank to build a five-star hotel to replace the aging lodge, we were asked to join the project.

This partnership presented the irresistible opportunity to create Taiwan's only five-star hotel located within a national park. We established our two companies' joint venture in 1991 and named it Grand Formosa Tianxiang.

In that era, the hotel business focused on scale, and Grand Formosa Tianxiang was no exception, boasting more than two hundred guest rooms. However, due to the hotel's location within Taroko National Park, its construction was challenged by complex regulations and approval processes. Construction vehicles were allowed to enter and exit the site only at night, which extended the construction phase to four years. Grand Formosa Tianxiang finally opened to the public in 1997.

My father and I at the groundbreaking ceremony for Grand Formosa Tianxiang in 1993.

To boost revenue, we broadened the hotel's customer base. We accepted group tours, hosted youth camps, and offered short-term promotions. But with average room rates hovering just above NT$3,000 (around US$100 in 2000), it became a constant struggle to balance income and expenses.

The hotel looked and felt more like a transplanted urban property—with multiple restaurants and indoor amenities better suited to a city. We catered to popular 1990s pastimes—such as karaoke, bowling, and card games—but guests could easily find those in Taipei without the long drive to the spectacular national park. What they truly came for was the natural beauty of Taroko Gorge—and by failing to meet that emotional need, we saw room rates stagnate for over a decade.

Inspired by the concept of the Aman General Hotel Management (GHM) resort, we repositioned the hotel under our Silks brand in 2009. Renaming the hotel Silks Place Taroko allowed us to think bigger and consider the entire Taroko National Park as our market versus just the Tianxiang Recreational Area. We understood that creating a genuine resort-style hotel in this world-class gorge required creating something that is immersive with nature.

Nestled within the national park, Silks Place Taroko gives vibrant expression to the stunning Taroko Gorge, with its picturesque mountain ranges, the gurgling Liwu River, trails with breathtaking sunrise and sunset views, playful Formosan rock monkeys, and serene star-filled nights. We hoped our guests would relax and connect with nature in a way that encouraged internal dialogue.

To bring that vision to life, we set out to completely redefine the hotel's structure—inside and out. We reimagined the exterior, upgraded all public spaces, redesigned every room type, and overhauled both the physical infrastructure and service systems. Every change was guided by a single principle: Align the guest experience with the character of the surrounding landscape.

We drew inspiration directly from nature. Sunlight, mountain water, stone, and wood were integrated into the design to mirror the spirit of the gorge. Floor-to-ceiling windows opened up to dramatic vistas, while interior elements subtly reflected the current season. The result was an atmosphere of understated luxury and elegant comfort—quietly inviting guests to feel both at ease and deeply connected to the land.

The transformed Grand Formosa Tianxiang was renamed Silks Place Taroko in 2010. The hotel's exterior design, public spaces, and room types—as well as its hardware and software facilities—were redefined and upgraded to blend harmoniously with the surrounding landscape, reflecting the beauty of Taroko Gorge. (The picture shows the outdoor poolside movie theater, offering breathtaking views of Taroko Gorge.)

To maintain a balance between business operations and environmental conservation, the number of guest rooms was reduced from 220 to 160. The 114 standard guest rooms are each about forty square meters. The top floor retreat presents a "hotel within a hotel" concept, with every two standard rooms combined to create a suite. Like Regent Taipei's Taipan floor, this floor also has an exclusive lounge and reading room.

Transforming an existing hotel is usually more difficult than opening a new one, because it requires more effort to shift old impressions. When Silks Place Taroko opened in 2010, it was weighed down by considerable burden from the past, and raising the room rates from NT$3,000 to NT$5,000 required a lot of hard work and adjustment.

In terms of marketing, Silks Place Taroko has focused on creating an experiential strategy to attract more customers. One of the hotel's first initiatives was to expand sales channels, including TV shopping platforms, and to offer discounts and package tours to travel agencics. The goal was to generate positive word-of-mouth marketing by providing customers with the opportunity to experience the new Silks Place Taroko.

Despite these efforts, the hotel still faced a challenge in attracting visitors who summarized the natural beauty of Taroko Gorge as "spectacular mountain scenery, but boring." Getting to the hotel also required an hour-long drive from Hualien Railway Station or the airport. We decided to turn this disadvantage into a unique advantage by creating rituals that give our guests the sensation of returning to their mountain home. Every process, from booking to shuttle service, contributes to this sense of delighted anticipation.

Aiming to give the area a new reputation as "spectacular mountain scenery, and fun," we established a recreation department focused on creating a cultural platform that's both local and unique and combines cultural innovation with a human touch. Our aim was to create an unforgettable experience that would make guests want to come back again and again.

Silks Place Taroko offered a wide range of experiences—from ecotourism and guided hikes to yoga classes, family crafts, and quiet courtyard evenings under the stars. Guests could swim in the rooftop pool, relax by the firepit, or gaze out over the valley from the fitness center. Indoors or out, the design always led back to nature.

But what made these experiences meaningful wasn't the variety—it was the way they revealed the place. Our staff members became storytellers, trained by local elders and Taroko National Park guides to share indigenous culture and ecological insight. Guests didn't just visit Taroko; they felt it.

At night, the valley came alive with open-air films, interactive performances, and the warm glow of late-night snacks in the lounge. On festival days, we created themed celebrations—especially unforgettable Lunar New Year experiences that blended tradition and joy. Starting in 2012, we gradually raised room rates and reinvested every dollar into improving the guest experience. That steady, back-to-roots transformation helped us triple our average rates over the next decade—proof that emotional connection is good business.

Resonance Through Place

Silks Place Taroko and its sister hotels, including Silks Place Tainan, Just Sleep, and Wellspring by Silks, share a commitment to local cultural resonance and environmental sensibility in their design. At Just Sleep hotels, guests are treated to an experience beyond a simple place to rest their heads. Each hotel's design is carefully crafted to be reflective of the location and community, promoting a connection between guests and their surroundings.

For example, Just Sleep Kaohsiung Zhongzheng, situated near the National Kaohsiung Center for the Arts, integrates music themes into its design. Just Sleep Taipei Ximending showcases its local street culture through its graffiti-style art walls and offers a free tour of the surrounding area with a large 3D map in the lobby. It also incorporates kaleidoscopes, neon lights, and other visual elements to connect its retro cultural roots with Instagram-friendly experiences. At Just Sleep Taipei NTU, blackboard walls in the rooms create a playful college atmosphere with scientific formulas and quotes reminiscent of its campus location. Interestingly, a professor who stayed there helped correct calculus formulas on the blackboard.

The newest addition to the Just Sleep family, Just Sleep Tainan, is located in a cultural and creative park that was once an old sugar factory during the Japanese colonial era. Its exterior is shaped like sugar crystals, and interior elements are inspired by sugar factories and ancient drums. The hotel is located next to the famous Ten Drum Cultural Creative Park, featuring taiko drum themes and experiences.

Each Just Sleep hotel meets the demands of a young clientele with its Instagrammable setting for guests to capture and share on social media. This proactive approach not only satisfies consumer demand but also generates positive word-of-mouth marketing for the brand.

Our newest addition is the Wellspring by Silks Beitou, which opened in September 2024 in the most popular hot-spring destination in Taipei after nearly three years of meticulous planning and construction. With the rising popularity of staycations and urban getaways, its strategic location near Xinbeitou MRT Station, with access to pristine hot-spring resources and panoramic views of Yangmingshan National Park, positions the resort as a key attraction for international travelers and local visitors inside Taipei city.

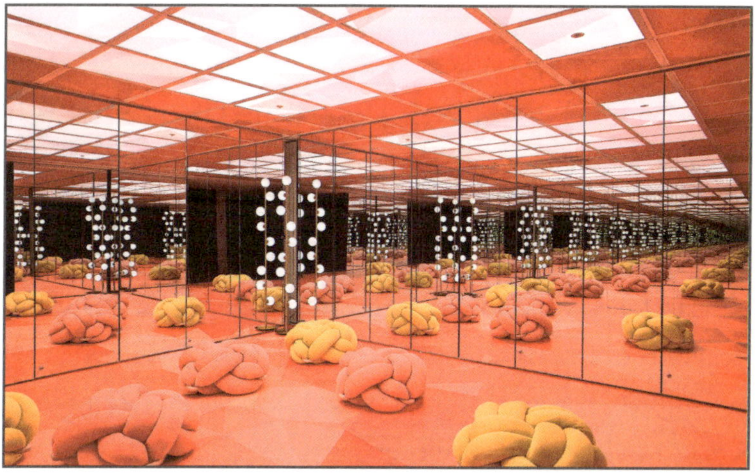

Just Sleep Taipei Ximending first opened in 2009, just steps away from the vibrant Ximen shopping district. After a refresh in 2019, the hotel added more playful elements to its design and collaborated with local artists to capture the energy and charm of Ximen. The above image shows how the hotel transformed its dark rooms into Instagram-worthy photo-op spots for guests.

Just Sleep Tainan, which opened in 2021, is situated in a cultural and creative park that was an old sugar factory during the Japanese colonial era. The first of its kind in Asia, this unique hotel has a drum theme permeating the entire building. Its exterior is designed to resemble sugar crystals, and the interior elements are inspired by sugar factories and big drums, making for a truly immersive cultural experience.

Wellspring by Silks Beitou has earned the prestigious EEWH (Ecology, Energy saving, Waste reduction, and Health) certification and is recognized as a gold-level green building. The hotel exemplifies sustainable development by addressing key areas such as biodiversity, green coverage, water retention, daily energy conservation, carbon-footprint reduction, waste management, indoor air quality, and water treatment. Guests can immerse themselves in a luxurious yet environmentally conscious setting—a "living" green structure that aligns with world-class sustainability standards, enhancing both the guest experience and societal well-being.

Every element of Wellspring Beitou was designed to reflect the land it rests on. The resort's rare green sulfur springs—acidic, therapeutic, and long revered—connect directly to Beitou's legacy as a hot-spring destination during the Japanese colonial era. Working closely with local artists, we wove this history into a space that honors both tradition and innovation.

The design draws on themes of spring, mist, rock, weave, soak, and pattern. Guests arrive through a grand entry framed by lattice towers that blur the line between inside and out. By day, green hills fill every view; by night, the glowing facade becomes an elegant urban lantern. Inside, soft stone walls and mirror-like black floors recall flowing water, while lanterns and screens offer quiet moments of stillness. The result is more than a hotel—it's a living expression of Beitou's past and Taipei's future.

SHG's newest addition, Wellspring Beitou, is an urban hot-spring resort located in Taipei. The hotel offers one hundred elegantly designed scenic rooms and suites that feature private hot-spring baths and cold-plunge basins. Additionally, the hotel has sixteen private bathhouses, public hot springs, an outdoor pool, a kids' area, an award-winning Wellspring spa, and an art gallery and lounge space showcasing local artists.

Wellspring Beitou's public bath houses incorporate Japanese-style landscaping, creating a tranquil setting for guests to enjoy their hot-spring experience.

Innovation with Roots

Hotels are more than just a place to stay. They are also a canvas for creativity and innovation. We treat them as platforms for exploring all kinds of possibilities, which has allowed SHG to claim many market-first innovations. In particular, our commitment to understanding the needs and preferences of our guests made us one of the first five-star hotel groups to launch outside catering and restaurants to connect with consumers beyond the hotel.

Among our most representative outside ventures is Silks Palace, which we launched at the National Palace Museum in 2008. More than a restaurant, Silks Palace is a cultural and culinary platform that truly captures the essence of Taiwan's rich history and heritage.

If Silks Place Taroko taught us that hotels could integrate with the environment and local community, then Silks Palace shows how culture and cuisine can come together to create a space where history, art, and food coexist in perfect harmony.

Converted from what was originally the employee cafeteria for the National Palace Museum, Silks Palace was designed by Kris Yao of ARTECH and interior designer Yukio Hashimoto as a world-class culinary and cultural destination. It is a masterpiece among Hashimoto's notable works in Regent Taipei, including Silks House and the renovated Robin's Grill and the Brasserie.

Situated on the west side of the National Palace Museum's main hall, Silks Palace was designed to blend seamlessly into its classical surroundings while reducing environmental impact. The minimalist glass exterior—modeled after the crackled ice glaze of Song-dynasty porcelain—captures reflections of the surrounding mountains, trees, and museum buildings. At night, the restaurant transforms into a glowing jewel box, its soft interior lights shimmering through the glass. Though this "glass house" concept

A view of Silks Palace at the National Palace Museum. Understanding the "why" is the key to unlocking the "how" for moving from excellence to transcendence in the case of SHG.

Silks Palace features a "cracked ice lattice" glass wall throughout the entire structure to reflect the mountain, forest, and National Palace Museum during the day. At night, it transforms into a dazzling crystal box that emanates the radiance of cultural heritage, designed by master architect Kris Yao.

doubled our construction and electricity costs, we chose to prioritize humanistic values over profitability.

From the start, our vision for Silks Palace has been to create a restaurant that celebrates culture as much as cuisine. Every design element, dish, and detail draws inspiration from the museum's collection. The crackled ice pattern reappears in decorative latticework and table dividers. Towering light columns echo the shape of the jade *cong*, a Neolithic ritual object. Hanging lanterns reference the *zhong*, a clapperless bronze bell once used in Western Zhou dynasty ceremonies.

We also paid tribute to iconic Chinese art. Scrolls, such as *Along the River During the Qingming Festival*, *Orchid Pavilion Preface*, and *A Palace Concert*, appear as murals, frosted glass, and paper-cut motifs. The result is a space where modern design techniques bring traditional forms to life—not as nostalgia but as living heritage.

Before the COVID-19 pandemic, more than half of our guests came from outside Taiwan. We saw this as a chance to showcase the best of Taiwan to the world, rooted in Chinese culinary traditions. The layout recalls a classical guesthouse, with an open dining hall on the first floor and ten private rooms upstairs—each named after a master artist from the museum's collection.

We created the Imperial Treasures set menu as a tribute to the museum's most iconic artifacts—dishes inspired by works of art like the *Jadeite Cabbage*, the *Meat-Shaped Stone*, the *String-Patterned Cauldron*, and the *Imperial Treasure Box*, reimagined as delicate sweets that mirror their savory counterparts. The knowledgeable members of the food-service staff gladly regale guests with the stories behind each dish in Chinese, English, and Japanese. It's a perfect complement right after the museum visit.

These culinary creations began as a passion project led by restaurant director Mandy Yang. Working closely with the Regent Taipei team, she curated dishes inspired by iconic museum pieces and historical banquets. Her deep love of history and meticulous attention to detail shine through in every course.

Mandy combed through countless archives and ancient texts to reconstruct the imperial dining experience. She collaborated with chefs to develop menus aligned with major exhibitions, thus introducing immersive dining experiences such as the Kangxi Imperial Feast, the Manchu-Han Imperial Feast, the Qianlong Imperial Banquet, the Southern Song Dynasty's Gourmet Cuisine, the Confucius Feast, and the Daqian Banquet.

Her dedication to cultural accuracy has drawn praise from scholars—including the former director of the Beijing Palace Museum, who dined at Silks Palace with Qing-dynasty experts and later invited Mandy to conduct further research in Beijing.

The Creative Mindset

Observation and creation are two values that have an impact beyond the confines of traditional fields of study, offering a way of looking at the world that is both innovative and practical. Observing our environment, economy, history, and culture gives us insight into how we can create a better future. But observation and creation need not be limited to these areas of study; they can also be applied to dialogue and innovation.

We often think of innovation as creating something new—but sometimes, the most powerful ideas come from seeing old things in a new light. In Japan, the concept of *reuse* goes beyond recycling objects. It's about reimagining their purpose—giving new life to what already exists.

At SHG, we have embraced this mindset not just in materials but also in strategy. One example is how we extended our F&B expertise beyond hotel walls, launching stand-alone restaurants that carry the same quality and creativity into new settings. Reuse, in this sense, isn't just a sustainability practice—it's a form of creative thinking.

Regent Taipei's success story began with the simple idea of expanding beyond the hotel's physical space. Wishing to create new business opportunities by utilizing our accumulated expertise in food and culture, we broke away from traditional settings to set up independent restaurants in department stores.

Our focus on our culinary expertise paid off as we brought our five-star cuisine to air, sea, and land—in other words, airplanes, cruise ships, trains, and double-decker buses. During the pandemic, we quickly adapted to the changing market with Take Regent Home, offering fresh-cooked dishes, semi-prepared meal kits, fresh vegetable boxes, refrigerated steaks, and shabu-shabu products for take-out ordering. The resounding success of this move ushered us into the home-delivery market.

But this was not the first time that Regent Taipei had created a new market beyond the hotel. We set the precedent back in 2013 with our Champion Beef Noodle Gift Set, which became a market leader.

The idea for Champion Beef Noodles began in 2013, when we explored launching an off-site restaurant at the airport to raise Regent Taipei's visibility. We faced tight constraints: limited kitchen space, high rent, and a fast-paced customer flow. Efficiency wasn't optional—it was essential.

We looked for a signature dish that could deliver flavor, speed, and brand recognition. The answer was clear: beef noodle soup. At the time, we served two versions at Regent Taipei—one made with American beef at Azie in the first-floor atrium and another using Taiwanese beef at Lan Ting, our private twenty-first-floor restaurant. Both had a devoted following.

Regent Taipei COO Simon Wu had been involved in our F&B evolution since joining Regent Taipei in 2000, and he came up with the idea of drawing attention to Regent Taipei's beef noodle soup by entering it in the Taipei International Beef Noodle Festival. In fact, Simon didn't tell me his plan in advance, in case our noodles didn't do well in the competition; winning was essential to the promotion of our beef noodles.

The main challenge was that the competition required using Australian beef—a departure from our usual recipes. Early attempts by Regent Taipei's Chinese kitchen team didn't produce a broth that met our standards. Then, our French chef stepped in, experimenting with Western techniques to bring out the flavor in the unfamiliar cut. That cross-cultural collaboration led to a breakthrough.

The result was a triumph: Our team won the championship in both the Creative and Clear Broth Beef Noodle categories and took second place in the Traditional Braised category at the 2012 Taipei International Beef Noodle Festival. The win gave us a platform to promote Regent Taipei's beef noodles far beyond the hotel. They appeared on cruises, flights, trains, and even reached Hong Kong. CNN even called them a destination dish worth flying to Taiwan for.

Although our airport outlet eventually closed, our ready-to-eat beef noodle packs found new life during the COVID-19 pandemic. With more than one hundred million sold, they helped drive revenue at a critical moment and gave us the momentum to rebuild.

In time, we shifted away from operating restaurants in malls. At one point, we had concept restaurants—including Wasabi Japanese Buffet, Champion Beef Noodle, Spice Market, and Just Grill—in various spaces, such as Taipei 101 and the Eslite Spectrum shopping mall. But outfitting costs and short-term leases made the model hard to sustain. Today, we see greater long-term value in partnerships, such as our Spice Market inside the Indigo Taipei Hotel.

For Regent Taipei, reusing and reimagining in the world of restaurants mean not only branching out on our own but also bringing in the best from around the globe. A notable example is our commitment to collaborate with international guest chefs as curators of food culture and to serve as incubators for international brands seeking to establish themselves in Taiwan.

When Regent Taipei invited Andre Chiang to be its guest chef for three consecutive years, it inspired us to create Taste Lab, a hub for food, creativity, exchange, and experience that provided guest chefs with a low-risk trial environment to test the market and customer needs before officially opening their own restaurants. One of the guest chefs, Paul Lee, was the first to test his restaurant concept for three months at Taste Lab before launching his now-Michelin-starred restaurant, Impromptu by Paul Lee, in the Regent Galleria.

People often ask me about the origin of Regent Taipei's Haipai Shaved Ice, a dessert that appears only in private rooms or catered banquets serving ten to twenty people. Traditionally, Chinese banquets have offered eight-treasure rice with taro paste, but in the hot summer, people crave something refreshing. As a Kaohsiung native, I loved shaved ice served with various toppings and thought it would be a great shared dessert. The word *haipai* is a Shanghainese term for spectacular generosity. We felt it applied perfectly to the mountain of refreshing deliciousness that is our special shaved ice summertime dessert.

The Haipai Shaved Ice—a towering, playful take on a traditional Taiwanese dessert—was created by Chef Tsai Kun-Zhan, known affectionately as "White Nose," the former head catering chef at Regent Taipei. He piled the dessert volcano-style into a transparent, flower-shaped glass dish sixty centimeters wide and weighing nearly seven kilograms.

Regent Taipei invited world-renowned chef Andre Chiang as guest chef, starting in 2011, annually until his return to Taiwan to open restaurant RAW in 2014 and now Raw Culinary Academy.

The shaved ice is topped with around twenty seasonal ingredients, including fruits from across Taiwan: Jiufen taro balls and sweet potato balls, Alishan *aiyu* jelly, Wandan red beans, Jiasian taro, Taichung tapioca pearls, and Sanyi grass jelly. Served with dry ice to create a misty, theatrical effect, the dessert became a summertime sensation. In 2021, our Take Regent Home campaign launched a smaller version designed to serve four to six people—and it quickly sold out.

But innovation isn't always about scale. Sometimes, it's about mindset. Observation, after all, is a form of open-minded listening—and Haipai Shaved Ice reflects that creative curiosity. In hospitality, unlike tech, experimenting with new ideas requires only basic ingredients. That freedom allows us to think big, start small, and fail fast.

We've embraced that playfulness across our offerings. There's the Elvis sandwich—stuffed with peanut butter, bananas, and ham—and the oversized ostrich Easter eggs filled with sponge cake and served with colored pens for guests to decorate the eggs. If something doesn't work, we simply scrap it and try again.

We've also developed a pop-up incubation model that helps international brands enter Taiwan. Regent Taipei has hosted boutique names such as Lady M from New York and Hokkaido's Tsubaki Salon, home of the famous fluffy pancake. We provide more than just space—we offer marketing, PR, logistics, and sourcing support, giving these partners the tools they need to succeed in a new market.

No description of incubators is complete without mentioning Regent Taipei's success as the "capital" of international luxury brands in creating an unparalleled shopping and hospitality experience at the Regent Galleria. More than thirty years ago, in 1990, Regent Taipei embarked on a revolution in the Asian hotel industry by combining the hotel with a luxury boutique mall, which was the first Duty Free Shoppers (DFS)–concept Galleria in the world. All of the international luxury brands—such as Chanel, Hermès, Dior, Harry Winston, Bvlgari, Boucheron, Chaumet, Cartier, Tiffany, and Graff—established their first Taiwan outlets in Regent Galleria.

The operation of Regent Galleria effectively transferred to Regent Taipei in 2010, when DFS withdrew from Taiwan's market. Regent Taipei seized the opportunity to expand boutique shops from B1 to B2 to replace the former DFS store, creating a luxury lifestyle destination that also houses some of the best Michelin-starred restaurants and bars in Taipei.

The Regent Galleria sets itself apart from other shopping malls by providing tailored VIP services that utilize the group's resources in food, lodging, and travel. Our personal shopping VIP team can arrange private viewing, gift deliveries, lifestyle advice, and hotel concierge services to cater to the needs of individual guests. We also offer bespoke international gourmet travel experiences to our top spenders in the most sought-after destinations and restaurants around the world.

Despite the challenges of the pandemic, Regent Galleria's revenue more than doubled, and membership grew by 40 percent. Our top one hundred members spent more than NT$1 billion per year. Many VIPs who couldn't travel overseas shifted their spending to Regent Galleria, and some major brands saw their revenue double and triple from 2020 to 2023.

In 2022, Lion Travel and Regent Taipei teamed up to bring travelers a unique and unforgettable experience aboard Taiwan Railways' luxury train, Moving Kitchen. Taiwan's first gourmet dining car was where we applied the concept of "repurposing" Michelin-starred cuisine for travel.

Designed by Johnny Chiu of Taipei-based J.C. Architecture, the luxurious black and orange train features wide windows revealing the breathtaking scenery of the Taiwan coast, accompanied by elegant music and delectable local delicacies made with fresh ingredients. The Moving Kitchen Journey is a gourmet food tour around Taiwan featuring the finest cuisine from our group. The journey passes through Hualien, where the Silks Place Taroko team takes over, and Tainan, where the Silks Place Tainan team provides support.

To ensure a seamless dining experience, the train features a team of about twenty butlers and chefs, led by Group Executive Director of Development Riki Saito. The banquet division, Robin's Grill, and dining services teams all work together to create an unparalleled experience for guests. This is a very popular outing for our staff because they get to see the most beautiful parts of Taiwan, despite having to maintain perfect balance cooking and serving on the train.

Taiwan Railways and Lion Travel plan to introduce sleeping compartments in the near future, and Regent Taipei's butler team will be on hand to create a hotel-like experience on board.

This is just the latest example of Regent Taipei taking its offerings on the road. The hotel's famous Beef Noodle Soup was served on All Nippon Airways in 2012, then offered on a cruise ship in 2018 and on a Taipei sightseeing bus in 2021. Now, it can be enjoyed on Taiwan Railways' train, The Future.

Hotels can take any form, changing with the progress of human civilization. Who knows? Perhaps someday, Regent Taipei will travel to outer space to host interstellar travelers! The possibilities are endless.

Designers, Visionaries, and Icons

The Embodiment of Regent: Ralf Ohletz

Ralf Ohletz, former president of Regent Hotels & Resorts, played an integral role in expanding the boundaries of SHG through a fusion of cross-disciplinary DNA, resulting in a new business model of hotel and luxury residential complex development that became the brand's second line. I first met Ralf before the opening of The Lalu resort in Sun Moon Lake, which was designed by my favorite architect, Kerry Hill. With many interests and friends in common, Ralf always invited me to chat over dinner when he visited Taiwan. After I acquired the Regent Hotels & Resorts brand in 2010, I invited him to serve as the Regent group's president.

Ralf, whose full name is Ralf Ohletz Count von Plettenberg, is a descendant of German nobility, with extraordinary taste to match. He is an aesthetic concept artist who has worked with top architects, artists, and designers worldwide, as well as an antique collector who loves choosing unique artifacts from bazaars to use in hotel decoration. Before joining Regent, he had worked on prestigious projects including The Setai in Miami, The Datai in Bali and Langkawi, and the first Aman resort Amanpuri in Phuket. Ralf had been working and living in Asia for nearly forty years when I met him, and as a prime example of modern yet timeless, he became my mentor in conceptualizing hotel design. In fact, I was lucky to meet Ralf just as the luxury hotel group GHM, where he had worked for nearly thirty years, was changing ownership. Otherwise, he might not have wanted to make the switch.

GHM was founded by Adrian Zecha, former partner of Regent International Hotels and founder of Aman Resorts. Since the establishment of GHM in 1992, its brand DNA has been closely related to that of Regent and Aman, so when Ralf Ohletz joined Regent, he felt as if he had been working for the brand his entire life. He brought the group an international design perspective as well as the concept of hotel-residential development, both of which have had a lasting impact on our hotel group to this day.

Regent Taipei has always been a mixed-use complex. We were the first hotel in Asia to include a luxury boutique shopping mall, and under Ohletz's leadership, the group also opened the "first" mixed hotel-branded residence in Europe in Regent Porto Montenegro, mentioned earlier in this book. From its initial offering of eighty-eight rooms to the completion of its fourth phase with three hundred sold-out units, the property commanded premium sales prices of 10 percent to 15 percent per square meter over nonbrand comparable units, a testament to its strong market appeal.

Ralf took thc Regent-branded residences to a new height in Regent Phu Quoc, where we reimagined a new generation of hotel residences with a flexible layout villa concept. We introduced the first Sky Villa, where each hotel suite is endowed with a swimming pool on the balcony with panoramic views. We also created a flexible room mix in each villa, so a three-bedroom villa can also be split up into three separate rooms and a suite to maximize yield for owners. The result was that the entire inventory of forty villas and forty Sky Villas was sold out during the pandemic, with complete payback to our development partner, BIM Group, as the resort opened in 2022.

Wellspring by Silks Jiaoxi, located in Yilan, incorporates the concept of brand and local culture by collaborating with the art world. Hosting resident artists throughout the year, it has become a cultural platform for promoting the beauty of Yilan.

All SHG hotels incorporate local characteristics into their building and interior designs. For instance, Silks Place Tainan welcomes guests with representations of Tainan's drumming culture.

The lobby of Silks Place Tainan showcases a modern yet classic interpretation of traditional cultural heritage. Inspired by the architecture of the Confucius Temple, the latticework displays the beauty of traditional architectural design.

Paying Tribute to a Master Designer: Yukio Hashimoto

The Japanese master interior designer Yukio Hashimoto, who collaborated with Regent for twenty years, passed away in 2022. He was my idea of a true master, with diverse designs ranging from high-end restaurants to five-star hotel interiors such as at The Peninsula Tokyo, as well as furniture, lighting fixtures, and art installations. Each of his works was a modern classic that left a timeless impression. Reexamining his work through the decades, I find that he surpassed himself with each successive project and evolved over time.

After I acquired control of Regent Taipei in 2000, the first renovation project I undertook was the Chinese restaurant on the third floor, then known as Lan Ting (now Silks House). My goal was to create a modern Chinese restaurant where the customer experience was interwoven with classic Chinese calligraphy that bridged global aesthetics while also breaking away from traditional calligraphic expression. Our group executive director of F&B development at the time, Saito San, introduced me to Mr. Hashimoto, who was already a renowned restaurant designer in Tokyo.

I still remember the day that Mr. Hashimoto brought his model to Taiwan; we immediately hit it off. His concept was to create a restaurant that transported customers into an immersive world of frameless calligraphy. I admired his empathetic incorporation of art and culture into the dining experience, resulting in the award-winning Silks House.

Mr. Hashimoto was not only responsible for the design and renovation of all of our restaurants but also created another masterpiece, Silks Palace. The architect, Kris Yao, was in charge of the architecture, while Mr. Hashimoto handled the interior design. My only requests were that all design elements be related to the collection of the National Palace Museum and that the first and second floors reference the traditional concept of an atrium guesthouse. When I saw the model for the first time, I was struck by its beauty, particularly the central courtyard with its lamp pillars shaped like the traditional jade cong. Mr. Hashimoto taught me to reimagine culinary culture, and I am grateful for the aesthetic nourishment he brought to us.

Designed by renowned Japanese designer Yukio Hashimoto, Silks Palace opened in 2008 as a unique platform for food and culture. It not only serves as a restaurant but also showcases the perfect integration of museum collection and cuisine.

CHAPTER 6

Leading from Within

At Regent Taipei, we don't just hire talent—we cultivate small bosses. These are team leaders who think like owners, act with empathy, and lead by achieving results. By nurturing that spirit, we help our people grow into the best version of themselves in every facet of life.

Returning to Taiwan in June 1991, I was a twenty-six-year-old eager to make my mark in the world. Six months after I became VP of Regent Taipei, I was presented with the opportunity of a lifetime: Chairman Chen of Tuntex and Regent Taipei offered me the role of president, taking over from my brother Roger.

Roger brought extraordinary energy and insight to the role. Before becoming president of Regent Taipei in 1990, he had built a name for himself as a journalist, media entrepreneur, and later as a real estate investor and major antique collector. When I joined the hotel, I dove into every aspect of the operation and didn't leave the property for a full month. Roger was right there beside me. I loved that time with him. A night owl by nature, he'd inspect the storage rooms in the middle of the night—sometimes catching missing abalone and seafood that had quietly vanished from inventory. He wanted to focus more on his own Mainland China investments, hence the opportunity for me to step up to the role.

As the new president, I faced a multitude of challenges. Regent Taipei was managed by the global Regent group, but the board of directors expected the president to execute strategic plans, develop partnership projects, and prepare for an IPO. The chairman, Chen Yu-Hao, was a visionary who believed that hotels could benefit from the profit center system of his industrial Tuntex Group. Implementing this system at the Regent was my first daunting task, but I was up for the challenge.

While the profit center system is common in traditional industries and manufacturing, implementing it in the service industry, especially hotels, was a management revolution. Regent Taipei was the first hotel in Taiwan, and perhaps even in the world, to implement a profit center system.

Every management system comes with its own strengths and weaknesses. In the traditional hotel model, leadership is centralized. The GM is like the captain of a ship—authoritative and fully in control. While this structure supports quick decision-making from the top, it can also lead to inefficiencies among the staff. Over time, it fosters an "iron rice bowl" mentality—where bureaucracies and job security discourage accountability—and creates hidden costs that don't show up clearly in performance reports. Waste of food, energy, and other resources often goes unnoticed.

By contrast, a profit center system decentralizes operations. It treats each department as a separate business unit and empowers frontline managers to take ownership of their results. Adopting this model wasn't a small shift—it required wholesale organizational reform.

The F&B department offers a good example. Traditionally, all chefs would report to the executive chef, and the financial oversight of all kitchens stayed within that office. But under the profit center model, each restaurant became an independent unit with its own kitchen and financials. Now, chefs were accountable to the restaurant manager instead of the executive chef. This called for a complete redesign of reporting lines and job descriptions.

Like most five-star hotels, Regent Taipei operated with the executive chef overseeing all kitchens and the F&B director supervising all restaurants, so Huang and I started there—not as chefs, but as observers. We used operational management tools to map workflow, calculate time usage, and assess cost distribution for each restaurant. Those numbers helped us build a more transparent and accurate picture of performance across different outlets.

Implementing the profit center system turned out to be one of the most challenging experiences of my career. Resistance came from every direction—senior managers, chefs, even our GM.

As the system took shape, we transformed nearly every revenue-generating unit into its own independent profit center—we created more than twenty distinct units, each with its own staff structure, financial reporting, and bonus mechanisms tied to performance.

It was a bold shift in mindset: one hotel, many entrepreneurs. By organizing our operations into nested profit centers—each with financial accountability, autonomy, and clear performance metrics—we created a system that encouraged innovation at every level. This decentralized model wasn't just structural; it became cultural. Leaders began thinking like owners, and that shift in thinking seeded deeper transformations in how we led, learned, and prioritized.

The Discipline of Focus

The implementation of the profit center system at Regent Taipei gave me the opportunity to connect with its originator, Chairman Y. C. Wang, founder of Formosa Plastics Group and godfather of Taiwan industrialists. A native of Chiayi in southern Taiwan, Mr. Wang was serving as a government advisor on tourism development in Alishan and invited us to join him on a day trip to explore a potential collaborative project. Although that particular project didn't move forward, the experience made a lasting impression on me.

Mr. Wang was a man of few words, but when he spoke, each sentence carried weight. That day, he shared one insight I've never forgotten: To succeed in anything meaningful, you must focus—completely. It was a simple principle, delivered without fanfare, but it struck me with clarity. In the years since, that lesson has shaped how I lead and how I choose what to pursue.

That lesson on focus proved valuable during the Regent Taipei management contract renegotiations when Four Seasons took over the Regent brand in 1992. Regent Taipei seized that opportunity for a change in control to renegotiate the management contract into a simple licensing agreement with fixed value. After months of intense back-and-forth, Four Seasons proposed a price of US$10 million. We left the table—not out of frustration, but to reassess our position. I speculated that the proposed amount was probably the collateral value of our management contract that Four Seasons pledged for the bank financing, so the wiggle room was probably less than 3-5 percent for rounding error before they had to renegotiate with the bank. That evening, our chairman, Chen Yu-Hao, speculated aloud: "Their floor is probably 9.7 million."

The next day, we returned and asked if they would accept US$9.7 million. The negotiators were visibly surprised. "How did you know?" they asked. We hadn't known—we had simply listened closely, observed their expressions, and weighed their silences alongside their words. It was a moment that reminded me that empathy in negotiation is not softness. It's about perceiving the unseen constraints of others while maintaining clarity on your own objectives.

The principle of focus has become a central theme in the organizational learning we promote at our hotel group. The profit center system created a culture of going all out, but even with the best intentions, it's easy for important goals to slip behind urgent ones.

I've experienced this firsthand. Like many on our team, I've found myself so immersed in day-to-day demands that long-term priorities quietly fade into the background. On the surface, it may seem harmless—just deferring what's not urgent. But over time, neglecting these issues can obscure strategic risks, stall innovation, and diminish our future competitiveness.

It's the classic "boiling frog" scenario—not a failure of effort but a failure to stay mindful of what lies ahead.

In this context, the profit center model has done more than redefine our operations—it has reshaped our mindset. It has encouraged our team members to think like small bosses, embracing ownership and channeling focus toward what matters most while remaining grounded in our purpose.

When the COVID-19 pandemic hit, that mindset was put to the test. The disruption forced us to distill thirty years of hard-won experience—like brewing a high-pressure espresso shot. We had to let go of outdated habits, question the status quo, and quickly identify what still worked.

In the process, we emerged stronger—a more agile team built on mutual trust, shared purpose, and the belief that collaboration can carry us through even the most unpredictable storms.

Simon Sinek once said, "It's better to go slowly in the right direction than go speeding off in the wrong direction."[7] This perspective reminds us that progress is not measured solely by speed but

7 Simon Sinek (@simonsinek), 2015. "It's better to go slowly in the right direction than go speeding off in the wrong direction." Twitter (now X), August 13.

by the direction we choose. SHG cultivates a nurturing environment that celebrates the power of learning. We aspire to our hotel group becoming a learning organization where all members flourish together.

The hospitality industry spans a vast array of fields that transcend the traditional confines of tourism or hotel management studies. Formal education in these specific areas is not essential to enter the industry. We recognize that elevating Taiwan's tourism sector begins with education, and we categorize hospitality talent into two distinct groups: operations and business management. The current emphasis in hotel management education leans excessively toward operational aspects.

To bridge this gap, listening in on meetings of executive and group committees can be a transformative channel for growth for managers. As we immerse ourselves in these gatherings, day by day, a shared consensus and culture naturally evolve through osmosis. Meetings in our hotel group are notable for encouraging the participation of any interested colleagues, unless the matters discussed are of a confidential nature. One example of this learning culture is our weekly marketing and PR meeting. While the agenda centers on proposals, its true value lies in how we learn from one another. These sessions create space to observe presentation styles, exchange ideas, and share best practices across our hotel group. The strongest ideas often find their way into other properties—not by mandate but through mutual respect and inspiration. The ideas and proposals are constantly challenged in the meetings, and the mutual learning leads to joint creation.

At their best, meetings are more than operational check-ins—they're a form of collective learning. Colleagues who've attended meetings with me know that I expect active listening, thoughtful questions, and a constant hunger to learn. Ideas are challenged and refined to a level that exceeds everyone's expectations, and eventually, the process delivers optimal results.

From Small Boss to Big Boss

Every Thanksgiving, a special tradition takes place at Regent Taipei: the lighting of Taiwan's tallest indoor Christmas tree. The occasion was made even more memorable in 2021, as a group of esteemed colleagues gathered to take part.

Among the distinguished attendees were Regent Taipei Managing Director & Group COO Simon Wu; Group CFO Dick Lin; GM of Just Sleep and Wellspring and Group VP of Operations Cindy Chen; GM of Silks Place Tainan and Group Chief People Officer Rebecca Lee; GM of Silks Place Taroko Jackie Chao; and Ellen Chang (group executive director of marketing and communications). Our former COO and Chief Development Officer Venessa Koo also joined the tree-lighting ceremony.

I was immensely grateful to these individuals, who had stood by me during the challenging times of the pandemic. Their unwavering commitment saw them working tirelessly as they rallied their colleagues toward our common goals. Together, we achieved remarkable milestones, such as the transformation of Regent Taipei into an urban resort hotel, the establishment of the Take Regent Home take-out and delivery platform, and the successful digital transformation of our group.

What I've learned over time is that my energy is best channeled toward in-depth discussions with a select few rather than toward managing a large number of people. I recognized that my strengths were not in operations management but in identifying and empowering people who excelled at managing others. It is no coincidence that the current group of GMs within our organization has risen through the ranks via the profit center system.

Simon Wu's journey at Regent Taipei has been nothing short of extraordinary. He joined us as assistant manager of the Gallery Lounge bar. It didn't take long for his talent to shine. Over the years,

Simon moved wherever he was needed—managing the Brasserie, opening our off-site restaurants, serving as assistant F&B manager and then as GM of the F&B division, and ultimately rising to GM and managing director of Regent Taipei and COO of SHG.

His business instincts have guided bold decisions—including the repositioning of the Regent Galleria mall, an area outside his original expertise. But what defines Simon most is his business-savvy yet empathetic leadership. During the darkest days of the pandemic, he rallied the team, experimented with new models, and led by example. Under his leadership, the success of Regent Taipei ensured that SHG became the most profitable hotel group in Taiwan, paying record bonuses and dividends. Simon continues to lead both our flagship hotel and SHG with the same dedication and focus.

Cindy Chen also holds a foundational place in our company. Hired as the second employee of Regent Taipei, she became the first person to ever work as GM of three of our brands—Silks Place, Wellspring, and Just Sleep.

She joined us in 1988 as a GM's secretary during the hotel's construction phase. From the moment Regent Taipei opened, Cindy's ability stood out. She rose quickly through reservations, front desk, and other managerial roles. After gaining outside experience for a time, she returned in 2007 to help prepare and lead our new Just Sleep and Wellspring brands.

Cindy's deep knowledge of Regent culture, combined with her personal drive, made her the ideal leader to help shape new ventures. Alongside her professional growth, she has pursued personal development with equal energy—running marathons and earning an executive MBA.

We've also been lucky to welcome back many exceptional people who left to grow elsewhere. One of them is Rebecca Lee.

Rebecca began as HR manager at Regent Taipei, then worked at other hotels before I invited her back to serve as the opening GM of Silks Place Tainan in 2014. Under her leadership, the hotel turned a profit in its very first year. That same team later orchestrated the wedding of Taiwanese supermodel Lin Chi-ling—a signature moment for the property.

Rebecca brought bold ideas to the table. She created a one-stop wedding service that drew from local resources and reimagined what a hotel could offer. In 2021, amid pandemic constraints, she opened Just Sleep Tainan—and it turned a profit within three months.

Her path has been anything but conventional. She taught English before entering the hotel industry. And yet, time and again, she's proven that creativity, courage, and perseverance are what truly drive a hospitality renaissance.

My experience in hiring GMs has taught me that established hotels can benefit from outside hires, while the process of opening new hotels requires an infusion of the brand's distinct DNA. In essence, long-time veterans are ideally suited to open new hotels.

In 2017, a significant vacancy opened up for GM of Regent Chongqing—a new flagship Regent hotel that had just opened. Unfortunately, issues had developed between the hotel's owner and the originally appointed GM—who was not affiliated with Regent—prompting the search for a new leader capable of infusing the brand's essence in this new venue. After an extensive candidate selection process, our Managing Director Mark Keith recommended Melvin Yang, who, at that time, was GM of Regent Taipei and had relevant experience, having turned around Regent Beijing and Silks Place Taroko. Melvin's journey within the group began as business manager of an off-site banquet venue, Bando Club, after which he was promoted to business director, overseeing the group's off-site restaurants. In 2011, he assumed the role of GM at Silks Place Taroko, making him the youngest hotel GM in the industry at that time. Melvin's strategic leadership successfully transformed Silks Place Taroko from an unprofitable establishment into one of the leading resorts in Taiwan.

Following Melvin Yang's tenure, Jackie Chao, who joined the hospitality industry from a career in broadcasting, took the helm as the GM of Silks Place Taroko. Jackie's trajectory within the group was characterized by a steady climb, starting as director of marketing for Silks Place Yilan and then joining Silks Place Taroko, first as director of marketing and later assuming the GM role. Under Jackie's guidance, Silks Place Taroko has firmly established its presence in the region, continually enhancing the range and quality of its service offerings to become the most sought-after resort within Taiwan.

The name of one of Regent Taipei's restaurants reflects the importance our hotel group places on leaders who are committed to internalizing the group's vision, building consensus, and guiding their team members toward success.

When we renovated Regent Taipei's signature steakhouse and our teppanyaki restaurant in 2002, we knew it was time for a new name and identity. Traditionally, restaurants are named after the head chef or owner—but I had something else in mind.

"Let's call it Robin's Grill."

Robin Liu (1949–2015) was the legendary maître d' of the steakhouse, a walking encyclopedia of Western cuisine in Taipei. He had joined us when the hotel opened in 1990 and we had brought the legendary steakhouse concept over from the Hong Kong Regent. Robin was a hands-on manager with an unwavering focus on discipline and fundamentals. His leadership helped shape a generation of hospitality talent—among them, our current COO, Simon Wu.

Simon often recalls two lessons he learned from Robin:

"The first was extending hospitality to everyone, from VIPs to regulars—every guest got his business card. The second was consistency. Robin kept the same schedule every single day, even on New Year's Eve. That kind of discipline is essential to hotel operations."

Robin's Grill quickly became known as the West Point military academy of Regent Taipei—a tribute to the strong foundation of leadership and mentorship he built. Most of our best restaurant managers came out of Robin's tutelage, and his servant leadership is the benchmark of the group.

To me, naming the restaurant after a colleague who had grown with us from the ground up felt deeply meaningful. Robin Liu remains an enduring symbol of what we value most: dedication, humility, excellence, and service. He may be the only maître d' in the world to have a five-star restaurant named in his honor. Although he passed away before the pandemic that so severely tested our group, his spirit lived on in the standards he set—and in the resilience we drew from them as we came through stronger than ever.

Regent Taipei marked Thanksgiving 2021 with a Christmas tree–lighting ceremony centered around the theme of gratitude. I invited Dick Lin, Jackie Chao, Simon Wu, Cindy Chen, Rebecca Lee, Venessa Koo, and Ellen Chang to join me onstage to light the tree to express gratitude and appreciation to all their cherished colleagues.

Many talented individuals have emerged from humble beginnings within SHG to ascend to prestigious positions. Their diverse backgrounds include roles as bartenders, secretaries, assistants, English teachers, and radio hosts. It has made me appreciate the inclusivity and diversity within the hotel industry, which values passion and dedication over mere technical qualifications. We firmly believe in nurturing individuals who have an innate passion for hospitality and transforming them into empathetic leaders in our organization.

As we repositioned Regent Taipei into an urban resort, a fascinating revelation unfolded. A gracious and polite doorman initially assigned to welcoming guests emerged as an ideal activities director for the rooftop infinity pool. Likewise, members of our front desk staff renowned for catering to international elites demonstrated their prowess in handling energetic children. These discoveries led our group to proactively encourage our colleagues to broaden their skill sets and seek diverse learning opportunities.

We eagerly await the discovery of further talent among the treasure trove of our staff.

Regent Taipei, known for its openness and inclusivity, holds a distinct preference for nurturing passionate individuals and cultivating a multitude of small bosses from within its ranks. (Photographed at the 2014 Regent Taipei Alumni Association)

Since its launch during the pandemic in 2020, Regent Taipei Cruise has offered a variety of exclusive itineraries, including Buy NT6000 Get 6000 to indulge in gourmet delights, the Simulated Tokyo Holiday Cruise, the Twin City Holiday, the Halloween Fun Cruise, the Double-Decker Christmas Bus Tour, and the Six-Restaurants Food Extravaganza, ensuring an array of delightful experiences for travelers.

Amid the challenges posed by the pandemic, the Take Regent Home platform emerged as a shining star, elevating Regent Taipei to new heights. Offering exquisite five-star hotel cuisine through take-out and delivery services, this global e-commerce platform flourished into a promising growth avenue for the hotel's future. The remarkable success of this endeavor stands as a testament to the unwavering dedication and collective efforts of Regent Taipei employees, who banded together to create a miraculous achievement amid adversity.

CHAPTER 7

Legacy Through Sustainability

I began my career at Regent Taipei after working on Wall Street, where the focus—often the only focus—was maximizing financial value. That mindset shaped how I approached the hotel's major financial crises in the early 2000s: first fighting for control of the property and then navigating the global travel collapse after 9/11. My attention was fixed on the bottom line, doing whatever it took to protect investor confidence and maximize shareholder value.

As the stories in this book should have made clear, however, my approach gradually evolved over the course of subsequent challenges, each of which could have brought us to our knees but instead made SHG stronger, more resilient, and, most importantly, more humane.

As we approach the end of this book, I want to draw all the threads together to emphasize the core lesson I have learned with Regent Taipei and SHG, which is that empathy is the key to sustainability and resilience in business. This learning has transformed my management practice into a life philosophy.

Many corporate leaders overlook the differences between business skills and philosophy. The business skills I acquired in my MBA education and then put into daily practice demonstrate their advantage in the ordinary course of business—but if they remain at the level of technique or practice, they may prove inadequate at addressing major challenges, especially those on a global scale. In particular, a business that fails to establish its relevance to consumers and society becomes extremely vulnerable and ill-equipped to weather major crises or disasters.

Seasoned entrepreneurs and business leaders understand the importance of focusing on a business philosophy that involves constantly questioning, considering, and expressing the meaning behind what we do. In the words of the acclaimed Japanese business legend Kazuo Inamori, "Effective leadership requires noble thoughts and a life philosophy. Steering a triumphant business venture requires meticulously deliberating upon one's thought processes, worldview, and philosophical mindset."[8]

Inamori believes that a thriving business requires cultivating talented people with a common philosophical viewpoint that will serve as a foundation for making judgments and taking action. Adopting empathy as our business philosophy has propelled SHG to continuously evolve, turn crisis into opportunity, seek transformation in times of adversity, and channel innovative thinking at challenging junctures.

Have you ever wondered why charcoal-grilled steaks and seafood are always able to stimulate our appetites with their irresistible golden-brown hue and alluring aroma? The answer lies in how sugars and proteins react to high-temperature cooking—a phenomenon known

---

8 Inamori, Kazuo, *A Compass to Fulfillment: Passion and Spirituality in Life and Business* (McGraw-Hill, 2009).

as the Maillard reaction. This remarkable chemical process creates a symphony of flavors and intensifies aromas that tantalize our senses.

Sudden crises are like being thrown into a high-temperature environment. Rather than being seared by these conditions, we can use them as catalysts for our personal Maillard reaction, infusing our lives with richer flavor and vibrant color.

The COVID-19 crisis produced my personal Maillard reaction. Facing the real possibility of financial collapse awakened a whole new level of sensory perception in me. Instead of teetering on the abyss, I saw an opportunity to have a real impact, not only on the lives of my SHG family but on the broader hospitality industry as well. This insight allowed me to take a leap of faith that, against all expectations, brought outstanding business results.

Robert H. Burns, Regent's founder and the first chairman of the World Travel & Tourism Council, understood back in the 1990s what many are only beginning to realize today: Travel and tourism may be the world's most sustainable industry. It achieved racial and gender equity in employment earlier than many other sectors and has long served as a ladder of social mobility for marginalized communities. Its ecosystem ranges from small street vendors to global corporations, sourcing goods and services from local farms, fisheries, and artisans. It also plays a vital role in protecting cultural heritage—from the pyramids to UNESCO World Heritage sites. Unlike factories, which can be relocated, a hotel—or a historic monument—remains rooted in place, contributing to the local economy and safeguarding history and nature alike.

Recognizing that our hotels operate within this powerful framework of sustainability, we've made it central to everything we do. Our guiding principle—the golden rule—extends not only to people but also to the environments and communities around us. If we wish to be treated with care and respect, then we must offer the same to our ecosystems. That, to me, is the heart of sustainability. And it was the COVID-19 pandemic that made this connection unmistakably clear.

During the early days of the pandemic in 2020, when the hotel industry around the world was devastated by lockdowns and border closures, millions of hotel workers were laid off and unemployed. Like other hotels, Regent Taipei and SHG faced heavy losses and the burden of payrolls, and we faced the same questions of how to survive economically.

I often return to one conversation with my father, held a decade before. In his final years, he dedicated himself to giving away his entire fortune to philanthropy. He told me he had come to Taiwan with nothing and that he wanted to give everything he had gained back to Taiwan before he left this world.

I was overwhelmed by his generosity and couldn't imagine ever living up to that standard. But he shook his head. "As a frail old man," he said, "all I can do is write checks. But you—you still have your strength. True giving is to give your body and soul to lead people and make a positive impact on their lives. The hotel industry is a special one. It hires all kinds of people in need."

At first, I didn't quite understand his meaning. A luxury hotel is hardly a charitable concern, after all. But he explained, "Hotels hire all kinds of people, especially disadvantaged and minority groups who use their income to put their kids through college and transform the lives of future generations. This is what actually makes the hotel industry so special and sustainable."

At the time, I felt only a faint sense of deeper purpose—just a trace of something larger than myself. My father's words lingered in the background, comforting but distant. But in 2020, as I faced the impossible task of crafting a pandemic contingency plan, those words came roaring back. His call to serve—not with wealth but with presence—gave me the courage to do what felt unthinkable: implement a no-layoff policy at Regent Taipei and SHG, even as the rest of the industry unraveled around us.

That decision became our moment of truth. If we ask for loyalty from our colleagues, shouldn't we return it when it matters most? I realized then that my role in this business had never been just about numbers or control. It had always been about people.

What followed was more than just recovery—it was transformation. Our team members poured themselves into the survival of the hotel group with a new sense of ownership. They brought forward ideas, energy, and growth that carried us far beyond the crisis itself. When others faced staffing shortages when guests returned in late 2022, we were ready. Our early commitment paid off: By 2023, Regent Taipei had achieved record revenue and profit. What once seemed like a sentimental gamble turned out to be one of my best strategic decisions ever.

Rebuilding with Purpose

Following the widely reported April 2024 Hualien earthquake—when our team at Silks Place Taroko turned adversity into a case study in compassionate crisis response—we now face a different kind of challenge: renewal.

After the hotel being closed for nine months, our 2025 reopening centers on a new initiative: Retain and Rediscover. This program invites guests not only to return but to reconnect with the emotional and cultural threads that make Taroko not just a destination but a place of wonder, memory, and resilience.

But in fact, our dedication to sustainability dates back to the very beginning of our reconceptualization of Silks Place Taroko, when operating in a region that faces the constant threat of natural disasters, such as typhoons, earthquakes, and landslides, taught us the importance of respecting and adapting to the natural world. This thinking was a critical factor in our handling of the Hualien earthquake in 2024.

When local tourism experienced a downturn due to an earlier earthquake in Hualien (in 2018), Silks Place Taroko stepped up to support the entire mountain region's tourism industry and encouraged the return of visitors, helping local communities and farms survive this difficult time.

Silks Place Taroko focused on building the local economy by using local ingredients in our restaurants and ensuring that we maximized hiring from the local area, including many aboriginals. The hotel also promotes indigenous music and culture by inviting aboriginal performers and featuring indigenous music on its playlist. By sourcing locally and promoting certified products and sustainable procurement, Silks Place Taroko not only supports the local economy but also reduces its carbon footprint.

Now, with many trails in the national park remaining closed indefinitely following the 2024 earthquake, we are focusing on two main tours. The first is a tour of Hidden Valley, including the Xibao Farm that supplies the hotel with organic produce in season and the nearby experimental elementary school, which is the first forest school in Taiwan. The second tour is a stroll through the village of Tianxiang and nearby houses of worship that focuses on cultural history as well as on the mountain pathway and encourages guests to close their eyes and open their ears to the sounds of nature around them.

We've invited yoga masters as well as experts in Pilates, and provided singing bowl therapy and a range of fitness activities to enhance wellness programs for our guests. We've also launched our

Herbal Academy, where we introduce guests to our in-house herbal garden that supplies our kitchen and encourage them to raise their own plants to take home.

Finally, we've created activities under the slogan "Do Something for Taroko." The national park has assigned a team leader to teach our guests how to contribute to the healing of the park. One activity is building bee houses for solitary bees. The bee houses that guests make remain on the hotel grounds, but guests are always welcome to come back and visit their new "tenants."

Our new emphasis is on giving our guests a feeling of giving back to community and nature and educating them on why their participation matters, both in this smaller context and in the broader one. While full financial recovery will take some time, we treasure this opportunity to remake Silks Place Taroko as a model for more sustainable tourism.

The Pursuit of Happiness

I've come to believe that the true spirit of well-being quietly infuses everything we do as a hotel group. For more than two decades, we have championed the timeless principle of empathy and treating others as we would wish to be treated—a mindset that subtly influences the actions of ourselves and others.

Throughout the COVID-19 pandemic's severe impact on the hospitality sector, my unwavering stance was to embrace symbiosis with my colleagues, ensuring no layoffs. This mindset extended beyond our organization; I advocated for symbiotic relations between the government and businesses, urging wage subsidies to address the initial challenges.

Remarkably, our efforts were successful, as the government extended additional subsidies that enabled us to offer an array of comprehensive training programs that allowed innovative co-learning and cocreation initiatives to take root within our hotel group. At the same time, we extended a hand to unemployed tour guides, enlisting them to enlighten our teams about local cultures. Their need for income and our need for local cultural knowledge formed a perfect symbiosis.

Throughout this period, numerous international media outlets and organizations asked me to talk about Taiwan's successful pandemic containment and the transformative journey of SHG via Zoom and other video conferencing tools. Our participation contributed meaningfully to the collective welfare by aligning with our mission to bring the best of Taiwan to the world.

During the pandemic, I came to see more clearly the essential role of collaboration—among colleagues, with the community, and with society as a whole. I'll admit this hadn't always been my perspective. In my earlier years leading SHG, my focus had leaned heavily toward maximizing shareholder equity and financial performance.

But COVID-19 forced a shift. We had to reevaluate the balance of interests among stakeholders: our colleagues, customers, shareholders, communities, and the environment. In doing so, we began evolving toward a model of sustainability—one that recognized the deep interdependence between humanity, the earth, and the systems we rely on.

Some decisions were difficult in the short term. But the long-term outcomes proved that sustainability and profitability are not opposites—they can support one another. The two years of the pandemic became a defining period for us, offering the space and urgency to reshape SHG.

We emerged stronger, not by abandoning our core values but by doubling down on them. Those shared values, nurtured over time, helped us redefine our business and grow into a true hospitality powerhouse.

In the words of Regent's founder, Robert H. Burns, "The only thing we specialize in is luxury, and the only thing our hotels have in common is the fact that they are all unique." This uniqueness is the thread that binds all our hotels, and I firmly believe that our group will continue to craft unparalleled experiences that epitomize humanity's pursuit of well-being.

The crisis catalyzed our centrifugal cohesion and helped us recognize our uniqueness. This transformation molded us into a dynamic collective capable of learning, innovating, and collaborating synergistically for the greater good. Our SHG workforce had always kept up a rapid work pace, but transforming to survive the COVID-19 pandemic thrust us into overdrive.

Thinking of leadership as another facet of hospitality, I aspire to a future in which our hotel group improves performance by enhancing a sense of well-being among our staff. Fostering an environment where team members are passionately engaged with their work, are keen to learn and create together, and have a sense of mission and purpose is what will sustain our hotel group's long-term success.

I must emphasize that nothing we do will be an imposition on our guests. For example, from the ESG standpoint, providing bottled water in our hotels is ecologically unsound. Within the realm of hospitality, however, the convenience and comfort of our guests come first, and the truth is that access to bottled water is important to our guests, especially during outings in the hot summer months. While we implement ESG initiatives at the corporate level, we cannot force these principles on our guests.

Ten years ago, we began encouraging guests to have their bed sheets changed less often during extended stays as a means of reducing the environmental impact of the water, detergent, and heating consumed by laundering. Many of our guests had difficulty adjusting to this policy, and we didn't enforce it when we encountered pushback. Each of our hotels' GMs has the autonomy to decide how to balance business and environmental considerations, and we refrain from impinging on customers' rights and satisfaction for the sake of our own principles. Ultimately, the choice should be left to our guests.

The sustainability of our business becomes a reality through the endorsement of our customers. Well-being is not a creed but a lifestyle, and rather than insisting on being the first, our staff are primed to embrace these practices when the time is right.

Health-boosting tea and the detoxifying smoothies have become staples across Regent Taipei's restaurants, the Wellspring Spa, and the Tai Pan Lounge. Whole foods, fruits, and vegetables increasingly take center stage as our culinary offerings evolve—though we never impose any dietary preferences on our guests.

I have long dreamed of pioneering an intersection between modern technology and individualized wellness programs tailored through body scans and encompassing massage regimens, exercise routines, and personalized dietary plans. This wellness program holds exciting potential for our guests, and I hope to introduce it when the time is right.

In the past, valuing efficiency, I dedicated years to playing squash, which burns around one thousand calories an hour. The intensity of squash began to take its toll, however, particularly as age caught up with me, resulting in exercise-related injuries. More recently, I embraced Muay Thai, which expends around eight hundred calories per hour. The pandemic-induced hiatus prompted a reevaluation of my lifestyle and steered me toward swimming as the alternative sport during lockdown. This turned out to be the best thing I could have done for my aging body, as swimming involves whole-body stretching, cardio exercising, detoxing, and muscle and mental conditioning, all without impact. This combination of lifestyle adjustments has spurred a remarkable mental, physical, and spiritual metamorphosis.

A blend of ancient wisdom and digital precision: The AI-based traditional Chinese medicine (TCM) consultation system at Wellspring Spa helps guests reconnect with their bodies and build wellness habits tailored to modern life.

Weaving Well-Being into Life and Work

When I first introduced the concept of well-being within SHG in 2020, I focused primarily on physical health. But as time passed, I sensed there was more we could do. By 2022, a clearer definition emerged. True well-being, I realized, lives at the intersection of personal and corporate values—a wholehearted commitment to ESG that extends beyond business and into our homes and families.

With its focus on environmental, social, and governance principles, ESG offers a powerful framework for sustainable growth. It outlines not just what we strive for—but *how* we get there.

The pandemic rekindled my passion for the Regent spirit and deepened my appreciation for the remarkable people within our group. As we continue to pursue business benchmarks such as EPS, we've also embraced practices aligned with the UN's Sustainable Development Goals (SDGs): reducing environmental impact, strengthening corporate governance, and elevating social responsibility.

Hospitality, by its very nature, teaches us to live in harmony with our surroundings. We understand the value of long-term relationships—with communities, with ecosystems, and with people. At the heart of this journey is empathy. Time and again, it has quietly propelled our transformation.

Our commitment began with small, sincere acts.

We paired charity with celebration by adding a social mission to our events. We worked with community foundations to support job training for individuals with disabilities. In our hotels, we began repurposing half-used amenities and collecting leftover toilet paper rolls and toiletries and donating them to nursing homes in need.

Our group's dedication to public welfare has even extended to voluntary service. James Chen, the executive chef of Robin's Teppanyaki, serves as an example.

Dubbed the "Father of Teppanyaki," Chef James Chen joined Regent Taipei in 1993. His culinary skills quickly made him a favorite among politicians and business elites, and his signature teppanyaki fried rice—stirred and tossed with bacon, baby carrots, onions, garlic, eggs, and rice—has become a beloved classic.

But Chef Chen's influence goes far beyond the kitchen. He is also the driving force behind a volunteer group that supports the Taiwan Mennonite New Dawn Educare Center in Hualien. Leveraging his reputation, he has rallied a diverse circle of pilots, professors, doctors, lawyers, and socialites—creating a thriving community of hundreds of active volunteers.

James's life echoes the spirit of the Taiwanese ballad "Marching Forward." He left his rural hometown and a modest childhood—where iron wires and stones held down the family's roof during typhoons—for a new life in Taipei. At Regent, he found not just a career; he found fulfillment. That sense of gratitude led him to start Cooking for Love, a charity initiative that has quietly delivered kindness for years.

Through his leadership, SHG began sourcing eggs from the Dawn Ark free-range chicken farm, and we've encouraged our supply chain partners to do the same. The goal isn't just to support a worthy cause—it's to lead by example.

The humane treatment of animals matters. Factory hatcheries subject chickens to brutal conditions, but it takes only a little more to give them a dignified life. By choosing better practices, we're proving that compassion and business excellence can go hand in hand.

His example highlights how the hospitality industry serves as a force for good and promotes social mobility, offering vast employment opportunities that constitute 10 percent of the global GDP. Embracing both urban and rural landscapes, hospitality weaves a deep connection with local economies, nurturing small and medium-sized enterprises and individual ventures while fostering equality, championing the cause of the LGBT community, and striving for gender and employment parity.

This can be considered a key advantage of the hospitality industry. While many sectors grapple with integrating ESG practices and fret over the impact on their financial returns, the hotel industry effortlessly weaves an ESG ethos into its fabric because it is naturally attuned to the innate human quest for delight and contentment. At SHG, our mission of well-being embraces the fundamentals and focuses on sustainable approaches in our daily endeavors.

During the pandemic, we committed ourselves not only to protecting our employees, guests, and their families but also to supporting society more broadly. Our efforts went beyond physical safety to include mental, emotional, and spiritual well-being—embracing every facet of the human experience: family, food security, education, community, ecology, and culture. It was in this crucible that our vision of well-being truly came alive, weaving ESG principles, sustainability, and holistic health into something personal and lasting.

This belief carries through to how we lead. Whether you're guiding a team of ten or a hotel of a thousand, the job is the same: helping people thrive. One person at a time, one act of encouragement at a time, we build momentum. And when that positive energy flows across the organization, small daily choices become the engine of something much greater—well-being as a shared, living value.

Turning Purpose into Practice

The values we've long embraced—empathy, stewardship, responsibility—only come to life when they're translated into daily decisions. At SHG, sustainability isn't a slogan or side initiative. It's embedded into operations, design, procurement, and culture.

Regent Taipei's exclusive use of cage-free eggs reflects our commitment to ethical sourcing. The EcoMeet Sustainable Meeting package eliminates single-use plastics and integrates responsible sourcing into every touchpoint. Our Leftover Produce program turns surplus ingredients into curated dishes, reducing food waste while celebrating creativity.

Technology supports this mission. At the Brasserie buffet, the Winnow AI Food Waste System tracks and minimizes food disposal in real time. Even our rooftop herb garden serves a purpose—supplying chefs with ultra-fresh ingredients while reducing transportation emissions.

These are not isolated gestures. They are part of a coherent strategy aligned with the UN's SDGs and designed to improve not just performance metrics but the well-being of everyone we touch—guests, employees, suppliers, and the planet.

When done right, ESG is not an obligation—it's an invitation to lead by example.

This mindset—integrating purpose into practice—has reshaped how we think about hospitality across the group. One of the clearest examples of this transformation is Silks Place Taroko. What began as a modest, affordable lodging option evolved into a world-class luxury retreat—and more recently, into a model of sustainable hospitality.

That shift didn't happen overnight. While preparing for a 2021 speaking engagement on sustainable tourism, I reviewed our operations through the lens of the UN's SDGs and was struck by how much we had already done. In fact, many of our most meaningful changes predated formal frameworks. Our cross-departmental Corporate Social Responsibility Committee—established in 2014—had already been guiding efforts in governance, environmental sustainability, HR, food safety, supply chain management, and PR.

That realization didn't just validate our path; it deepened our commitment to sustainable thinking and reaffirmed the idea that true impact comes from internal alignment, not external pressure.

Far from the splendid natural environment of the Taroko Gorge, our hotel group has shown that sustainability can thrive even in the heart of Taipei's urban jungle. Regent Taipei became the first hotel in Taiwan to apply for certification by EarthCheck, a global leader in sustainability benchmarking for the travel industry.

When I spoke with EarthCheck's founder, Stewart Moore, he noted that most hotels take at least a year to earn silver status and five years to reach gold. Regent Taipei achieved silver in just six months. As he explained, this wasn't due to shortcuts—it was because sustainability had already been embedded in our operations for years. We weren't launching a new initiative. We were simply formalizing what had long been part of our DNA.

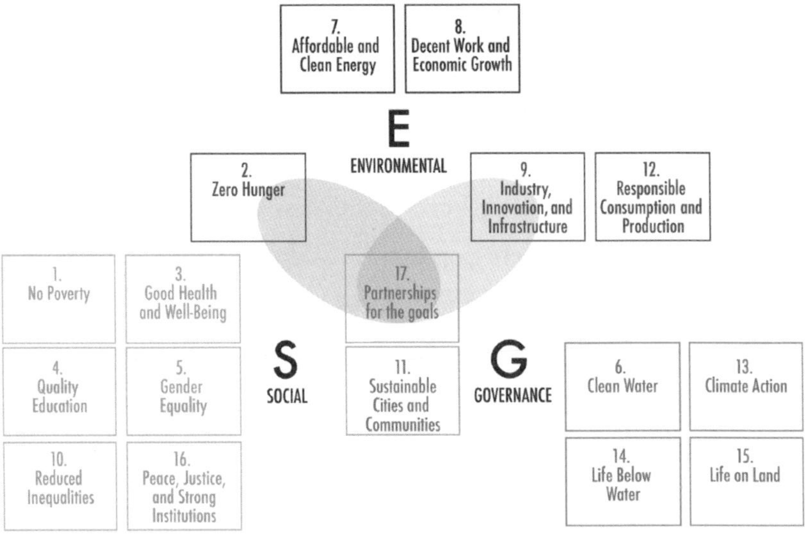

The UN's Sustainable Development Goals

Running a business is like embarking on an exciting journey into an unknown future. Too often, people become preoccupied with a change of scenery and overlook the importance of fresh perspectives. The transformative journey of the pandemic opened a new horizon that brought us an invaluable understanding of the importance of well-being and sustainability in terms of both individual happiness and greater human welfare.

This realization did not materialize out of thin air, however; it was rooted in understanding the complications of the past—something that often eludes us when all is going well. It is like the art of tea tasting, which requires a certain state of mind to appreciate the full complexity of the flavors.

To bring our vision of well-being and sustainability to life, I declared 2020 to be Regent Taipei's Year of Well-Being. Our approach wove sustainability into every aspect of our operations—from physical, mental, and spiritual health to family and community life, environmental and social responsibility, and ongoing learning.

The hospitality industry exists to craft experiences that spark joy and leave lasting memories. Whether through vacations, weddings, banquets, shopping, dining, or learning, our work touches people at some of the most meaningful moments of their lives.

That's why the guiding purpose of our hotel group has always been to "serve to move the world." It's a mission rooted in positive impact—by creating it for others, we find it ourselves.

Looking back, I realize that this aspect of our brand DNA began to emerge after the SARS epidemic.

The Wellspring Spa, occupying an area of five hundred square meters on the twentieth floor of the Regent Taipei, was the hotel's earliest venture into the realm of wellness. The lingering aftermath of the SARS epidemic prompted us to reimagine the hotel's purpose as more than a place for accommodation, dining, sightseeing, and shopping. Realizing the need to provide physical and mental rejuvenation as well, a spa seemed the ideal answer. We'd seen exceptional examples of the concept in Hong Kong's Peninsula Hotel and Bangkok's Mandarin Oriental. If we were to create a spa, it would have to be of that same caliber.

Rather than collaborate with existing spa-industry partners as most hotels do, we were determined to create our own spa brand that would reflect our global yet Asian heritage. We devoted US$2 million to planning, preparing, training, executing, and constructing our new spa. Finally, a fitting name was chosen—Wellspring Spa, inspired by a verse from "Nine Songs" in the ancient Chinese poetry collection *The Songs of Chu*—written more than two thousand years ago—which evokes imagery of water, fragrance, and brilliance.

With renowned calligrapher Tong Yang-Tze inscribing the name and Singaporean designer Franklin Po crafting the space, the element of water was artfully woven into the five senses of the spa experience.

We also enlisted the expertise of our Balinese aromatherapy consultant, Sofia, to curate treatments and train professional aromatherapists.

Wellspring Spa opened its doors in 2006 as a groundbreaking addition to the market. Nestled on the twentieth floor, it showcased eight single aromatherapy suites of forty-five square meters each, and two couple treatment suites measuring ninety square meters, each with a jacuzzi. Each aromatherapy suite included its own dressing, showering, bathing, and steaming facilities. Large platform daybeds were thoughtfully placed by the windows that offered captivating views.

The success of Wellspring Spa has been nothing short of remarkable, securing the World Spa Award for Best Hotel Spa in Taiwan at least seven years in a row. Believing that the spa is not just an indulgence within Regent Taipei but epitomizes a lifestyle of physical and mental serenity, we offer Wellspring's bath products in all SHG hotels. Following in the footsteps of Take Regent Home, which brought the essence of Regent Taipei's cuisine to customers' homes, the Wellspring Spa product line has also made its mark online, allowing patrons to savor the cherished Wellspring Spa experience in the comfort of their own homes.

SARS ignited the spark of the initial concept, but it was the COVID-19 pandemic that brought Regent Taipei even closer to connecting the dots. My Berkeley classmate Dr. Phillip Chang, a visionary practitioner of Traditional Chinese Medicine (TCM) and serial tech entrepreneur, had founded the Wenzhi TechTCM in Silicon Valley to employ the power of AI and big data analytics in the practice of TCM. I was captivated by the potential of this innovative approach and decided to introduce the AI TCM consultation system to Regent Taipei.

Our original goal was to offer health and wellness guidance to our colleagues, who were physically stressed during the pandemic—

and the results were overwhelmingly positive. Encouraged by that success, we extended the AI TCM consultation service to our VIP guests, who responded enthusiastically.

Seeing its transformative potential, we officially launched the AI TCM system at Wellspring Spa. We integrated personalized assessments with herbal-infused treatments and expanded our offerings to meet rising demand during the pandemic. This included wellness products such as tea bags, foot-bath sachets, and bath sachets, as well as aromatherapy solutions designed to support sleep, immunity, lung function, and detoxification.

In 2020, we began a remarkable transformation that reimagined Regent Taipei as five distinctly themed sub-hotels. On the twentieth floor, the focus turned to physical and mental healing, with Wellspring Spa on one side and a tranquil sky studio and spa suites on the other—each offering sweeping views of the vibrant city below.

Unlike conventional business suites, the spa suites exude a serene vacation ambiance with their soothing wooden flooring and the window area occupied by a low canopy bed instead of the usual chairs. Each bay window boasts a unique design featuring wooden screen doors that can be easily adjusted to control external light and sound. Our recommendation is to leave some gaps to allow gentle sunlight to filter in, finding this to be the most "well-being" way to start the day.

The inspiration for this setup came from the CEO of a top international bank. Despite traveling three hundred days a year, he always appeared sharp, energized, and well-rested. Having experienced the fatigue of frequent travel myself, I asked him what his secret was.

He told me that he exposed his head to direct sunlight each morning. That simple practice, he said, anchored his body's rhythm and restored his clarity. We carried this insight into the design of our spa suites by building the canopy bed into the window—inviting guests to greet the day by exposing their head to sunlight and begin their wellness journey with nature's first remedy.

The window bed serves a second purpose as a massage daybed. Our Wellspring Spa team has developed a gentle sleep therapy performed right in the bed, using pressure point massage across the eyes, head, shoulders, and neck. Once the treatment ends, the aroma therapist slips out silently, leaving the guest to drift into uninterrupted sleep.

For anyone who's struggled with insomnia—as I have—this isn't just a treatment. It's a gift. A deep night's rest can be the most restorative luxury of all. Not to mention the remedial exposure to the sun first thing in the morning.

For seven consecutive years, Wellspring Spa at Regent Taipei has clinched the coveted World Spa Award for Best Hotel Spa in Taiwan, showcasing an unparalleled ability to curate a lifestyle of relaxation that caters to both mind and body. From its captivating window views to its serene atmosphere, every element is carefully orchestrated to offer a holistic, five-senses experience that leaves guests rejuvenated and refreshed.

The Singular Value and the Five Spirits

In the quiet hours of reflection—usually after navigating another crisis—I began to see a pattern. Our transformation didn't follow a rigid playbook, but there was one singular core value that consistently helped us adapt and grow. It anchors everything we do and serves as our internal compass: empathy.

For our guests, we seek to serve them as we wish to be served.

For our colleagues, we seek to treat them as we wish to be treated.

For our shareholders and owners, we seek to run the business as owners would run it.

For our partners, we seek to deal with them as we wish to be dealt with.

For our environment, we seek to protect it as we wish to be protected.

Layered onto empathy are the five spirits: fusion, ownership, rooted innovation, sustainability, and well-being. They are less a doctrine than a rhythm—one that we return to every time we rebuild, rethink, or reimagine. Together, they form the scaffolding for our next evolution.

International Celebrities at Regent Taipei

Regent Taipei has hosted many world leaders and global celebrities, including former US President George W. Bush; former US Secretaries of State Condoleezza Rice and Mike Pompeo; singers Michael Jackson, The Three Tenors, Lady Gaga, Sting, Whitney Houston, and Beyoncé; sports stars Michael Jordan, Kobe Bryant, and Andre Agassi; superstars such as Tom Cruise and Keanu Reeves; renowned directors Martin Scorsese and Ang Lee; Japanese singers and songwriters Ayumi

Hamasaki, Rie Miyazawa, Tetsuya Komuro, and Namie Amuro; the South Korean K-pop bands BTS, TWICE, and BLACKPINK; orchestras such as the Berliner Philharmoniker and Vienna Philharmonic, and classical musicians Yo-Yo Ma, Itzhak Perlman, and Anne-Sophie Mutter; and Hong Kong stars Jacky Cheung, Andy Lau, and Joey Wong. Regent Taipei was even chosen by French director Luc Besson as an opening setting for his film *Lucy*, featuring Scarlett Johansson in the hotel lobby and suite.

The "King of Pop," Michael Jackson, held concerts in Taiwan in 1993 and 1996. The legendary actress Elizabeth Taylor joined him on the latter occasion, indulging in the classic Regent Cooler, a classic drink still served at Regent Taipei that was specially concocted for her.

Jackson's security team inspected Taipei's five-star hotels six months ahead of his visits, and both times they opted for Regent Taipei. We can categorically debunk certain rumors spread about Michael Jackson's preferences, such as bathing solely in evian water. Jackson was carrying out extensive tours at that time, often to developing countries, so he always brought an ample supply of mineral water. On one occasion, he didn't finish the evian he'd brought, so rather than waste it, he used it in his bath the night before he returned to the US, which is how this rumor began. He was grateful that Regent Taipei arranged for a small piano in his Regent Suite for private rehearsals.

True international celebrities often display genuine humility. Once, I unexpectedly encountered rock poet and The Police lead singer Sting at Regent Taipei's bar, and our conversation went on effortlessly for an extended time. After Mariah Carey gave a concert, she returned to the hotel and joined our chef in preparing a pasta feast as a heartfelt gesture to her hundred-strong crew. Whenever Celine Dion graced Taiwan's stage, she brought her entire family along. Her favorite spot? Robin's Teppanyaki.

I met French movie star Sophie Marceau when she assumed the role of international ambassador for luxury jeweler Chaumet and graced their brand event at Regent Taipei. Another illustrious figure, movie star Michelle Yeoh, has been a cherished friend of mine for three decades. We instantly connected when she was filming *Butterfly and Sword* in Taiwan in 1992.

It was Michelle's influence that spurred Luc Besson to choose Regent Taipei as the backdrop for *Lucy* ten years after his stay while promoting *The Fifth Element*. On this occasion, Regent Taipei's own staff became part of the movie, including VIP team member Jesse Hung, who had risen from Regent Taipei's first batch of butlers trained to provide personal service to global luminaries.

During the filming of the movie, I enjoyed a deep conversation with the great director over dinner with media magnate Madame Wang Shaw-lan. Having watched previous movies directed by Besson, I said, "Your films have a lot of violent scenes, but I've observed that the key to saving humanity is always a woman. Why is that?"

Luc Besson burst out laughing and replied, "My films are all about love." Rather than promoting violence, his creations often underscore a message of love with scenes of profound affection. Consider *Léon: The Professional*, focusing on a hitman's connection with a young girl. Likewise, *The Fifth Element* introduces Leeloo, a genetically crafted human portrayed by Milla Jovovich, and *Lucy* has Scarlett Johansson evolving into a 100 percent superhuman, transcending time with a message of love: "I am everywhere." Across human evolution, women embody infinite love.

In my own life, the embodiment of love and grace will always be my beloved wife, Constance.

EPILOGUE

A Philosophy of Hospitality

I once thought to myself, *You could have had a much easier life! Why did you borrow so much money twenty years ago to buy out a partner ten times more powerful than you and take over the management of Regent Taipei?*

On the public front, I was responsible for ensuring that Regent Taipei maintained the steady operations its employees and shareholders deserved. *Privately*, it was also a business my father had founded. Although I haven't matched his boundless generosity—he gave away his entire fortune—I've never been drawn to material wealth. From a young age, I've pursued wisdom and learning. I don't seek thrills or status. I find joy in seeing others happy.

It's been said that fostering happiness in others is a form of enlightened self-interest—that by advancing the well-being of your community, your own fulfillment follows. I've found this to be true. Bringing happiness to others has become my measure of success.

This book concisely encapsulates the past three decades, but the saga of SHG would have been much less riveting without the challenges it has faced. Adversity during the pandemic years drove our group's metamorphosis and resurgence, and I felt that I, too, gained a second lease on life.

The story doesn't end here; a new journey has begun. I believe in lifelong learning, and learning remains my lifestyle and my attitude toward life.

Celebrating Regent Taipei's remarkable three-decade journey coincided with a rebirth shaped amid the challenges of the pandemic, which reminded me of Laozi's metaphor: "He who is filled with greatest virtue and curiosity is like a baby."[9]

The idea is that our lives should have the kind of profound virtue that a newborn baby possesses. A baby's existence is profound because it is initially untouched by loss, but adulthood often distances us from authenticity and our inherent virtues. That's why returning to childlike purity becomes imperative, and during the pandemic, I came to appreciate the importance of giving new life.

The true journey of discovery is not about finding new landscapes but about gaining new perspective. I hope this story inspires you to see the world, and your place in it, with fresh eyes. As we move forward, may well-being serve as a foundation for a world built on mutual benefit, shared creation, and continuous learning.

Challenged to reflect, transform, and embark on a journey of discovery, what new perspective do you hope to gain?

Carrying On the Legacy with Gratitude

I cannot end this book before expressing my respect and appreciation to several people who have made crucial contributions to the development of Regent Taipei and the Silks Hotel brand.

---

9 Laozi, *Tao Te Ching*, translated by D. C. Lau (Penguin Books, 1963).

In particular, several key figures represent distinct chapters in Regent Taipei's narrative.

Regent Taipei's opening GM, Jean-Pierre Dosse, was the company's linchpin from 1990 to 2000. Starting out as corporate VP of F&B for Regent Hotels & Resorts, Jean-Pierre launched restaurants in several iconic Regent hotels before being promoted to GM of Regent Taipei.

Jean-Pierre Dosse and me

Having demonstrated his culinary expertise worldwide, Jean-Pierre created Regent Taipei's culinary genealogy and became the godfather of its outstanding gastronomic culture. A marathon enthusiast, he often took long runs between the hotel and distant locales such as the Yangmingshan and Neihu mountains that surround Taipei—an expression of the military-style discipline he applied to management and passed on to the next generation of group leadership.

The company's central figure in the first decade of the new millennium was CEO Amy Hsueh, who began her Regent Taipei journey at the front desk. Endowed with deep hotel operational expertise, Amy was about to leave the company to pursue her passion for interior design when our paths crossed serendipitously on a hotel staircase.

When I learned of her plans, I convinced her to join my project office to work on hotel design and development instead. Assuming the mantle of CEO at just forty-one, Amy led the launch of multiple new ventures—off-site restaurants and proprietary brands that include Just Sleep, Silks Place, and Wellspring by Silks. Her intuitive grasp of market opportunities spurred diversification and innovation across the group and expanded Regent Taipei's footprint beyond the city's center. Amy became the cornerstone of our second decade of advancement—a loyal and consummate leader second to none.

The third linchpin was Ralf Ohletz, a legendary figure who spent nearly three decades working alongside Regent partner Adrian Zecha, creator of the Aman brand. When I acquired the Regent brand in 2010, I invited Ralf to join as president of Regent Hotels & Resorts.

From 2010 to 2018, Ralf guided the group's international renaissance with vision and insight. As scion to a venerable German lineage spanning half a millennium, he taught me a great deal about design philosophy and aesthetics. Even more significantly, the new business model he introduced—centered on developing integrated hotel and residential complexes—became our blueprint for navigating the post-pandemic landscape.

Currently leading the transformation and operations is SHG COO Simon Wu. Simon originally joined Regent Taipei's Italian restaurant, Cafe Studio, during Jean-Pierre's tenure and later returned to manage the hotel's F&B department after gaining experience in the group's off-site restaurants.

Under Simon's leadership, the F&B program entered a renaissance, defined by collaborations with world-renowned culinary masters that helped reenergize Taiwan's dining culture. Beginning in

2018, he focused on building Regent City, a bold integration of the hotel and the Regent Galleria into a unified destination for accommodation, gastronomy, and luxury retail.

During the pandemic, Simon helped guide the team through a wave of innovation, giving rise to the Take Regent Home e-commerce platform and the land-based cruise concept—both of which expanded our vision of what hospitality could be.

Behind these influential figures stand two patriarchs who have steadfastly safeguarded Regent Taipei throughout its history. Trusted advisors to my father and my esteemed seniors, they've lent their wisdom and experience to our journey.

One of them is former CFO Dick Lin, who joined the company as cost controller in 1988 and became an expert in the company's back-office procedures, cost control, and procurement. For more than three decades, he was a steady force, guiding us through many challenges. A cornerstone of his legacy is the successful implementation of Regent Taipei's profit center system—an effort that owed much to his tenacity.

Although Dick formally retired in July 2022, we are fortunate to continue drawing on his wisdom. He returned to serve as my chief of staff and chair our Silks Place Taroko subsidiary, allowing us to benefit from his decades of expertise and dedication.

Another veteran is Gu Piao-Ping, who led our security department for many years. Formerly the chief of the Zhongshan police station, Chief Inspector Gu brought unwavering support and guidance to the team—a role that earned him deep respect throughout the hotel.

I also want to thank several other leaders for their invaluable contributions to Regent Taipei's success:

- Cindy Chen, VP of operations and GM of Just Sleep and Wellspring—and the second person ever hired at Regent Taipei

- Rebecca Lee, our chief people officer and GM of Silks Place Tainan and our southern regional operations
- Jackie Chao, GM of Silks Place Taroko, who partnered with Melvin Yang to reinvent the resort
- Melvin Yang, now GM of Regent Chongqing, also demonstrated his extraordinary turnaround expertise at Silks Place Taroko and Regent Beijing. Our former COO Venessa Koo rejoined the group after twenty years and helped us transition from Regent to a multi-brand development.

Our marketing and PR team, led by Ellen Chang, played a crucial role in navigating the turbulence of the pandemic with a strong digital transformation and media strategy. I'm also grateful to respected food critic Sam Yao for his thoughtful advice and encouragement over the years.

The inception of the VIP team in 2000—spearheaded by my former secretary Debbie Tai and GM secretaries Juno So and C.C. Chiang—was another key moment. During the SARS epidemic, this one-stop service model for our top guests accounted for 10 percent of our revenue.

Today, that legacy continues through the dedication of C.C. Chiang, joined by the exceptional Jocelyn Huang, and our master butler Jesse Hung, whose leadership of the Regent VIP services team helped drive our remarkable growth during the pandemic and beyond.

Looking back on this journey, I want to extend special appreciation to three respected elders with deep connections to Regent Taipei.

Foremost among them is Yung Hung-ching (1923–2022), honorary chairman of Shanghai Commercial and Savings Bank (SCSB). Even during our 2022 Zoom board meetings, Mr. Yung remained engaged and committed until the very end. A titan of Taiwanese banking, he was also a bridge between generations of financial development in Taiwan, China, and Hong Kong.

My family's relationship with Mr. Yung is long-standing. SCSB helped facilitate our joint venture with its subsidiary China Travel Service on Silks Place Taroko, but our bond went further. The bank supported my father's early ventures in shipbreaking in the 1960s, issuing letters of credit from its Hong Kong branch. When SCSB opened in Taiwan, my father became one of its first major clients. Even in our US investments, we stayed connected through SCSB's San Francisco branch.

Later, when a bank officer's widow urgently needed to sell her shares, my family agreed to buy them without hesitation or even asking the price—an act of friendship that made us shareholders.

Though based in Hong Kong, Mr. Yung maintained a special fondness for Taiwan and always stayed at Regent Taipei. Even when the bank once held its board meeting at a different five-star hotel, Mr. Yung and his wife quietly returned to stay with us after the first night out. During our renovation in the early 2020s, we carefully presented him with the redesign plan for his preferred suite, ensuring his comfort and welcoming his input. His insights helped us improve the experience for our older guests.

I once asked him during a call, "Since you have property in Taipei, why stay at our hotel?" He replied, "The property is an investment. Regent Taipei feels like home." He holds the record of more than two thousand nights stayed with us.

Mr. Yung's influence extended far beyond friendship. His leadership at SCSB and the bank's corporate culture became a model for the kind of family business we strive to build—professional yet accountable to owners. His legacy continues to guide us through our joint venture and his heir John Yung.

The second individual I must recognize is Henry Kao, chairman of I-Mei Foods. I first met Mr. Kao in 2000, when I was preparing to buy out Chen Yu-Hao's controlling stake. Mr. Kao, then representing Ta-An Bank, advised me throughout the process. Although we ultimately didn't secure a loan from the bank, our personal friendship took root and has only deepened over time.

We share the same birthday—though we were born more than ten years apart—as well as a love for classical music and thoughtful conversation. Mr. Kao has been like an older brother and a key figure in many of our strategic partnerships.

His support was instrumental in securing government aid for the hospitality industry during COVID-19. He also provided valuable guidance on our Taipei airport project, our collaboration with the Shin Kong Group on Jasper Villa Xinyi, and other ventures that continue to shape our future.

My first meeting with Minister Lin Chia-lung came about thanks to Henry Kao. At the very start of the pandemic, Henry asked what support the hotel industry might need from the government. Within days, he reached out to Ye Chu-lan, then-chairperson of the Taiwan Visitors Association, and arranged the introduction. That meeting with Minister Lin opened the door to crucial funding. Without Henry's quiet mediation, the pandemic would have dealt a far heavier blow to Taiwan's hospitality sector. That initial round of government support helped set SHG on its path to becoming a learning-focused organization.

The last of the elders I want to thank is Chen Yu-Hao, founder and former chairman of the Tuntex Group—and once my boss and chairman of Regent Taipei.

When I returned to Taiwan and became Regent Taipei's president in 1991, Mr. Chen had already built his Tuntex group into one of the leading conglomerates in Taiwan. He was a brilliant, decisive leader with a deep knowledge of economics, a talent for cutting through complexity, and a sharp sense of vision. He pushed for the Regent to become the first service-industry enterprise in Taiwan to adopt the profit center system, laying the business-savvy foundation we still use today.

In time, though, our priorities began to diverge. When our group went public in 1998, Mr. Chen remained focused on the interests of Tuntex, while I found myself defending the future of Regent Taipei and my own family. Our disagreements grew into open conflict. The final two years we worked together felt like two decades. And yet, that trial shaped my business experience more than anything else. I carry forward the lessons I learned from Mr. Chen with real gratitude.

In life, I am grateful to friends and family who support us but also to worthy adversaries who challenge us and make us stronger.

After thirty years of challenge and renewal, Regent Taipei enters its next chapter, not as a survivor but as a symbol of transformation. I hope our journey gives strength to others who are facing uncertainty in their own industries. I want to thank every member of our Regent family for their resilience, creativity, and commitment to our mission: bringing the best of Taiwan to the world—and the best of the world to Taiwan.

I am deeply grateful to my late parents, whose values continue to guide me; to my wife Constance, who has supported me quietly and unconditionally, allowing me to give my full effort into everything I do; and to my daughters Lauren and Kristen and son Alexander, who bring joy and renewal to my life.

I also want to thank the broader Taiwan society and the international community—our guests, partners, property owners, shareholders, and friends. You stood with us through the hardest times, and your trust has made everything possible.

May the story of Regent Taipei offer a little confidence, a little clarity, and a little hope—for whatever comes next. *Fiat lux*—let there be light!

ACKNOWLEDGMENTS

The journey of this book began not as a project, but as a process: one sparked by crisis, shaped by reflection, and sustained by the quiet persistence of many dedicated individuals who helped transform my experiences into words.

In April 2020, as the world stood still during the early days of the COVID-19 pandemic, James Wey of J.P. Morgan invited me to speak on a global webinar about how our team at Regent confronted the crisis. I shared our story about how we rose up, adapted, and led with purpose in the face of uncertainty. The overwhelming response to that webinar surprised me. It reminded me that our experience might resonate beyond the walls of our hotels, offering strength to others navigating their own storms. That realization planted the seed for this book and I am grateful to Mary Yang of Commonwealth Publishing Group of Taiwan for the initiation of the original Chinese edition."

My heartfelt thanks go first to Ching-I Lin, the author of the original Chinese biography published in Taiwan 2022, who spent countless hours—through the uncertainty of a global pandemic—attending Regent executive committee meetings, conducting interviews, and adapting the narrative through rapidly shifting business landscapes. Her commitment and care carried this book through to its completion.

To the Regent team, especially Ellen Chang and Dazy Chen, I am thankful for your artistic precision and patient effort in creating the visual elements that bring this story to life with design and grace.

I am indebted to Stacy Mosher, our translator, introduced to me by Shirley Lin. Stacy did far more than translate—she thoughtfully restructured the book from a biography into an autobiography, adding new reflections and context that enrich this English edition. Her deep understanding and editorial sensibility have shaped the voice of this work in meaningful ways.

Special thanks to Sammy Wong of Whale Capital and Peter Hung of Forbes Media Group for their generous support and encouragement, and for introducing me to the dynamic duo at Forbes Publishing—founder Adam Witty and chief publishing officer Evan Schnittman—whose vision and energy gave this project a renewed voice.

The team at Forbes Books has been a model of speed, professionalism, and heart. I am especially grateful to Shandi Thompson, my authority advisor, whose steady guidance kept this project grounded and focused. Thanks also to Joel Schettler, our thoughtful developmental editor who surgically rearranged the entire book for clarity and relevance; Matthew Morse for the simple yet elegant zen water garden cover design with symbolic double fish icon and Olivia Tanksley, whose care and coordination brought the manuscript into its final form; and to Elizabeth Brueggemann, our meticulous production editor who ensured all the moving parts are converging for final book publication.

To my wife Constance Chiang, thank you for your exacting comments during copy editing and, more importantly, for keeping me humble and grounded. Your quiet, unwavering support has allowed me to grow and do the best I can in everything I do.

To my daughter Kristen, who worked alongside me during the translation period, and to my dear friend Giang, who constantly reminded and challenged me to reimagine and stay true to myself throughout this journey—thank you both for your insight and presence.

I am deeply grateful to my late parents and grandmother, whose values continue to guide me; to Constance, who has stood by me with unconditional love; and to my children—Lauren, Kristen, and Alexander—who bring meaning and energy to my life every day.

– **Steven Pan**

ABOUT THE AUTHORS

Steven Pan is Executive Chairman of Regent Taipei and Silks Hotel Group, one of Asia's leading hospitality groups. A globally recognized entrepreneur and thought leader, he has led international investments, hospitality turnarounds, and multinational transformations with a commitment to cultural empathy and human-centered leadership. His experiences span decades of building global partnerships, navigating crisis, and promoting sustainable growth in competitive markets.

Based in Taipei, Taiwan, Steven is passionate about cultivating the next generation of resilient leaders. *Crisis and Renewal* reflects his belief in purposeful reinvention as the cornerstone of both business longevity and personal fulfillment. He is the founder of SR Pan Foundation in memory of his father. Steven is a Trustee of UC Berkeley Foundation and Cochair of Chancellor's Asia Council. He also serves on the Columbia Business School Board of Overseers.

Ching-I Lin holds master's degrees in Business Administration from National Taipei University and Gerontology from National Cheng Kung University. As a widely-published biographer and astrologer, she transforms abstract ideas into meaningful narratives and helps executive teams distill their core visions. For nearly two decades, she has explored entrepreneurship, brand strategy, and business models, working closely with executive teams to distill the essence of their vision.

ABOUT THE TRANSLATOR

Stacy A. Mosher is a Brooklyn-based translator, editor, and writer. A native of Michigan, Mosher lived in Hong Kong in the 1980s and 1990s and worked for more than ten years as a journalist in both Hong Kong and New York. Since 2007 she has been a full-time translator from Chinese to English, and has translated more than a dozen books and scores of articles by authors from mainland China, Hong Kong, and Taiwan. She is also an adjunct thesis advisor in translation at New York University.